Our Dream Was Canada

Order this book online at www.trafford.com
or email orders@trafford.com

Most Trafford titles are also available at major online book retailers.

Printed in the United States of America.

ISBN: 978-1-5539-5874-1 (sc)
ISBN: 978-1-4669-5812-8 (e)

Trafford rev. 04/11/2014

 www.trafford.com
North America & international
toll-free: 1 888 232 4444 (USA & Canada)
fax: 812 355 4082

Our Dream Was Canada

Escape from Czechoslovakia
with Two Suitcases, Children and a Dog

by
Eva Zidek

To my family: Petr, Kate, and Tom

Acknowledgement

I wrote this book as a person to whom English is a second language. Initially, I composed the text in Czech, then I struggled to translate it into English. My grammatical style is not perfect, however, I hope readers will understand and appreciate my experience. I feel that my intention to describe the journey of modern political emigrants is worth telling, despite imperfect language skills. Friends from the Bow Valley Literacy project helped me with corrections and, actually, they encouraged me to finish my writing and to publish it as a book. I would like to thank all of them, especially Madeline Crilley, who helped me enormously. My special thanks goes to Maruta Jacobs for editing, correction, and final preparation of my "loose" writing to make this book.

Contents

Preface

In the year 2002, our family had an anniversary. Twenty years ago we had decided to leave Czechoslovakia and make a new beginning in Canada. As I describe in my book, this decision did not start in young, foolish heads. We were in the middle of our careers, had children, and had never made such hasty resolutions. While Czechoslovakia, as an Eastern Bloc country, was not high on the economic scale, improving that side of life was not our reason for leaving. (Actually, the first years in exile are often harsh and many escapees sadly remember the "good life" back home.) Foremost, we suffered, as most citizens behind the "iron curtain," from increased limitation of personal freedoms and from our inability to fight back. Relationships among people in Czechoslovakia, after the 1968 Soviet occupation, worsened and we were shocked that we had to be careful of what we said, not only in front of strangers, but also with our friends, relatives, and even our children. The deterioration of the natural environment was, for us, the "last straw." Unfortunately for us, we had a better knowledge about environmental problems than the average citizen, who tended to view such problems as temporary or did not know about them at all. There was little hope of improvement under communist management in the 1980s and nobody could see any "light at the end of the tunnel." I, personally, fell into despair, with the question: "What next?"

At least, one thing was clear to us when we decided to leave Czechoslovakia. Our goal was Canada. With two children, a couple of suitcases, and our dog, we started our pilgrimage. First there was a holiday in Yugoslavia, then we spent over a year in a refugee hotel in West Germany. Finally, thanks to our sponsor, we landed in Toronto – Canada – in the fall of 1983.

The most important step, getting to Canada, was behind us. However, there were many important steps still ahead of us. First, we had to learn the language of our new country. We also had to comprehend the "psyche," the soul, of our new country. The language and culture of a people determine the subconscious relationship they have with their nation. (An example: If you hear a joke at home, you laugh along with everybody else. But did you ever translate a joke into another language? Often, even if you translate it well, you get only a polite smile.).

A high priority for us was to find work. Of course, we hoped to find jobs in our field, forestry. Disappointed, we found that our twenty years of foreign work experience did not count for much. Suddenly, we were like students, freshly out of school, looking for our first "Canadian" working experience. In the meantime, we had to take a job, any job.

We also had to find a place to live. Although our big wish was to live in the mountains, at the start we looked for jobs anywhere, except the cities, and lived wherever we found work. When Petr's work in north-western Ontario came to an abrupt end, we decided to change our approach: We moved to the Rocky Mountains in Alberta with only the hope to find work there, because that was where we ultimately wanted to live. Finding work was not always easy, but on the other hand, we were able to enjoy the beauty that only mountains can offer. As we both preferred fieldwork to office work, and we often did manage to find such work, our magnificent surroundings delighted us even more. We did not move again, which only shows, how much we liked it.

There was something else. From the time of our arrival in Canada, our goal was always to find not only refuge, but also a new home for our children and for us. It is, after all, a wonderful feeling to be happy with the place where one lives, especially, when a person has decided to move of their own free will. I guess we have managed this last step as well. It takes time to overcome the differences, to feel truly at home, but it is worth undertaking.

This book describes all our struggles. It tells how we became familiar with our new country – Canada – the place we chose when we left our original homeland twenty years ago to search for increased personal freedom, better environmental conditions, and beautiful surroundings in which to live, work, and raise our children.

1
Our Background

"[1970] an era of apathy and extensive demoralization; very gloomy times; people just consuming information without questions ... with every day the same." — Vaclav Havel

Our family's choice of Canada was spontaneous but taken with some knowledge of the country. This knowledge was reasonable for the level of detail accessible to the average citizen in Czechoslovakia, who did not want to arouse undue attention. Any interest in more information could bring the suspicion, "Why you are interested in Canada?" Probably we had our idea of Canada already, from our childhood, when we learned about the world and about a large country with a small population and enormous natural beauty: Canada with vast areas of forest, clear rivers, huge lakes, endless prairie and above all spectacular mountains. It was a place we dreamed of calling home. For Europeans, the aboriginal inhabitants, and their early history were a symbol of a free life in harmony with nature, as opposed to the life of "civilized man" who works to the destruction of nature and often feels in despair because of this.

We left our country, Czechoslovakia in 1982, when we had the feeling we couldn't breathe there any more. It was a conscious decision, taken by responsible adults with a young family.

In Czechoslovakia in 1968, after a violent end to the "Prague Spring" and the military occupation by the Soviet Army, many people, especially young ones, fled the country. It was the only time when the average citizen had the chance to get out. During the previous twenty years behind the Iron Curtain, obtaining a permit to travel out of the country was a complicated procedure. For most, leaving in 1968 was a protest against the Soviet invasion. When their tanks crushed Prague's airport and streets, it meant the end of any hope for democratic improvements in Czechoslovakia. The prevailing feeling was that whoever runs away is the winner. The world looked at it the same way.

Military invasions are viewed by the rest of the world with displeasure, even if the other countries are powerless due to international agreements. The Western countries opened their doors to the huge wave of refugees from Czechoslovakia and gave them advantages about which we, several years later, could only dream. We met some of the refugees from 1968 later, in Germany, and in Canada. Some did not seem to remember why they left their homeland. They did not appreciate what the new country offered them. We knew our reason for leaving very well and this knowledge helped us in the first difficult years.

My name is Eva and I was born and raised in Prague, the capital of Czechoslovakia. Though I liked the historical city of Prague, I wished to live in smaller place. I prefer nature and I felt like a prisoner in the city. In my childhood, our home with its large garden was situated on the outskirts of Prague. My fondest memories are of the moments when I sat on the window ledge, looking out to the garden and far-away forests and dreaming I was somewhere out in nature.

I chose forestry as my occupation. This was an unusual choice for a woman, especially if she has a small physique and does not fit the stereotype of someone who would choose to do "men's work." My parents were not very happy about my decision. They didn't permit me to study at the forestry college situated outside Prague. I had to carry my dream through high school to university.

Eventually, I started to do what I wanted, to study forestry and to be close to nature. I liked the school, the Prague Faculty of Forestry, not only for its university atmosphere, but also for its location. Due to some changes in organization, the forestry faculty was moved to a small town. For three of the five years, we lived in a sixteenth-century castle, surrounded by forest. This served as a field station for our university.

After finishing my studies, I started my forestry career on the borderland, close to East Germany in a place called Erzgebirge. It was exactly what I wanted. Like any young person who leaves a familiar environment, I had to pay for my new freedom with the feeling of loneliness, and even shock, due to meeting with an entirely new way of living. My schoolmates, my brothers and sister were not there, only strangers with their own problems. They were willing to gossip about each newcomer, especially a young female. However, I survived, and within a year I became a district chief forester. In the interior of Czechoslovakia, I would have had to wait years for the same position. To my knowledge only two other women in the whole country worked in the same position at that time. My office was in the area called "immigrant land." Originally, most of the inhabitants were of German origin. After World War II, the majority were forced to move to Germany. Since then, the land was largely settled on a temporary basis as people came for a couple of years and then left again. Nothing was fixed, built or renewed. The buildings fell into disrepair and the original rich pasture land was reduced to swamps because nobody repaired the previous laboriously-made drainages.

My district was situated on a mountain plateau at an elevation approximately 1000 metres above sea level, unusually high in Czechoslovakia (Prague is 350 metres). The centre of the district, where my office was located, was a deserted hamlet. Working on a temporary basis, were horse masters (some work in the forest was still done by horses) and some brigade workers. When I started my new position, the church was demolished, as it was beyond repair. My office was seven kilometres from the town where I lived. Like most people, I didn't have a car, but I used a small motorbike to get to work in the summer and skied to work in winter (which lasted nearly half of the year, due to elevation).

In spring 1968, I got a better position at the Forest District Konopiste, about thirty kilometres from Prague. I was glad that I could closely watch the events of Prague's "Spring." I was actually in the city when the Soviet tanks rolled over Czechoslovakia. For two days, I was unable to travel back to my district because the public transportation was suspended. I saw, first hand, the despair and broken hopes of my country, which after twenty years of suppression had begun to rise, due to renewed democratic life. However, this process was destroyed by the occupation by the Czech's "dearest friends," (the unofficial name for the Soviet Union in Czechoslovakia).

People started to leave from the first day of the occupation, but the spirit of the Prague Spring kept the nation together even more than before the aggression. We still had hope, but it slowly dwindled. I had to make an emotional decision, whether to run away as many others had done or remain because of my strongly nationalistic feelings. The latter course finally won. At the same time, Petr, a friend who was to later become my husband, also tried to make his dream come true, spending most of his time in the forest, observing wildlife and hunting. He obtained a position as a forest ranger in the mountainous part of northeast Bohemia, Jeseniky. Later we worked in the same mountains together. During the time of the Prague Spring he was trying to mend his unhappy marriage. He also went through feelings of leaving everything behind, but for him it was more of a fantasy, without any hope of fulfillment.

For the citizens of Czechoslovakia, the years 1969 and 1970 meant not only the gradual loss of any democratic advantages gained in 1968, but also a loss of their interest in political events. While in 1968, and after the invasion, there was still the opportunity to express opinions freely and to hear news without censorship, it only pointed to our hopelessness. Later, with the return of censorship, there was no way to find the truth and to show feelings about our country. Vaclav Havel wrote about this time in his memoirs, and I have quoted him at the start of this chapter.

For Petr and myself, personally, it was the start of our own "new" era. We were married and we hoped, as others do, that our life would be wonderful.

Meanwhile, I managed to have a political problem, which immediately cost me my job, my apartment in the forest district's government housing, and my security. In 1970, the government banned demonstrations on the anniversary of the Soviet invasion. They still occurred, but were broken up and all participants were cruelly treated by police. I foolishly applied for a holiday on the anniversary date. It was known I was from Prague, so my absence was immediately connected with the demonstration. My director in the Konopiste forest district had supported the political party which opposed the government before the Soviet invasion occurred. After the invasion, he turned 180 degrees and literally welcomed the Soviet tanks. I was also the only employee in the region who was not a communist party member. This provided another reason to get rid of me. My new job, which I found several weeks later, was actually better. However, I still remember this experience of desperately trying to find a job in Czechoslovakia, where unemployment did not exist, and to work was the law.

At this time, the word "freedom" was meaningless, so it was ironic that Svoboda, the surname of our president, meant "freedom" in Czech. Everyone tried to live and mind their own business. We closed our eyes to political matters. We did not watch news or read news-papers. Sometimes, we were so poorly informed that we did not know about road check-stops, which were announced ahead of time.

From Prague, we moved 250 kilometres to a hamlet with only five houses. On the positive side, we had jobs which we liked: Petr worked as a forester and I worked as an independent forestry biologist for a provincial park. We took advantage of country life and spent most of our leisure time out of doors. We raised dogs and chickens and had a horse for trips. Our circle of friends grew, or rather changed, to include those who liked this kind of life, shared our interests, and with whom we felt comfortable. Our children, first Kate, then Tom, occupied us within the "closed circle" which we developed around us.

The problems of our country and the mendacious politics of our government were widely acknowledged. It was a theme which friends talked, and sometimes joked, about secretly among themselves. The government pushed the slogan, hated by our generation, but unfortu-nately fulfilled: "With the Soviet Union, together for eternity." It was a slogan of slavery. We felt it when our small children, attending pre-school, had to join in various public anniversary celebrations: the 1917 Russian Revolution, our country's liberation from Hitler's occupation by the Soviets in 1945, and so on. The communist government never mentioned that the western part of Czechoslovakia was liberated by the Americans. Nobody was allowed to celebrate that.

I remember an amusing incident, when Kate mispronounced a conso-nant and with enthusiasm recited, "Lenin sewed" instead of "Lenin lived." But nobody dared to laugh aloud. So a time began, which I hated most, when we had to be careful of what we said in front of our children because they would be asked in school about their parents' opinions. Our children felt left out when we refused them permission to join the Pioneer organizations, but we disagreed with the philoso-phy and felt they served mostly for brainwashing. So far we had managed to postpone joining any public organizations, pleading travel difficulty due to our location, far from the village. But we knew, it would be only a matter of time.

Like others, we cursed the government, made jokes, and tried to keep our privacy. Certainly, there were enough things to be angry about. We lived in the north-eastern part of Czechoslovakia (North Moravia), where in each town, even in the little ones, a Soviet garrison was stationed. Our closest town, Jesenik, known for its spa and recreational opportunities, had a population of 10,000. After 1968, the population increased by 2000 Soviet soldiers. The city of Olomouc, which was a distance of eighty kilometres from us, had a strong garrison of about 250,000 Soviet soldiers. Nobody knew the exact numbers. However, we knew that Czechoslovakia paid all their expenses, their livelihood, training, transportation, and even constructed new apartments for their officers, although there was a desperate shortage of housing for Czech citizens. There were other, economic, problems. The international agreements, which were made in 1968 for the renewal of our economy, were abandoned. The new agreements were made only with the partners of the Warsaw Pact. Machinery in factories was out of date, supervisors were required to be communist party members but their lack of education was overlooked. Many commodities were so scarce that a trip to buy basic consumer goods was commonly referred to as "a hunt." Whenever the opportunity arose, people stole from the government.

The communist party was not only the leading party, it was the only party. There was no opposition in Czechoslovakia. The forest director in the North Moravian region was just one example of a communist party member who was not qualified for the position to which he was promoted. This man had only one year of forestry schooling, equivalent to an apprenticeship. Needless to say, his decisions were terrible. He often proclaimed that he, on behalf of North Moravia, would pay off all Czech debt by virtue of the sale of timber from this huge forest region. He did not know or care about forest management practices, sustainable yields, or allowable cuts.

Instead of having a classless society, our superior class consisted of the central politburo of the communist party. The heads of regional and district offices all had privileges of which the average citizen could only dream: high wages, travel opportunities, and many free services. The average citizen, wanting to travel to the West, had to first obtain a travel permit, then permission for a holiday from the work director, and finally currency from the bank. Only a few applications were approved annually. Inequalities existed in the education system also: the children of politburo members and those of communists had an open door to universities, irrespective of their marks in high school.

In the mid-seventies, as pollution began to have a greater effect on life in Czechoslovakia, the public soon began to suspect the quality of the food.

The privileged class began to establish chemical-free farming operations and to air-freight food from abroad for their own use exclusively. However, the nation paid for it.

The environment and living conditions became a frequent topic of discussion between friends. The bad news was never published, but some would occasionally leak out. The magazine *Young World*, published an article titled "Dinosaurs did not survive—what about us, people?" Various issues were raised, but the root problem, the incompetence and irresponsibility of the government, was not addressed. The official line was, "Everything in the country belongs to the working class"; government actions cried, "After us can come the flood!"

The first "ecological disaster," as it was later called, had occurred about twenty years earlier in the mountains on the East German border (Erzgebirge). I started my forestry career just to the south of this area.

While the north showed problems, the area where I worked was still covered with beautiful old forest. My district was an up-land plateau with vast swamps. Part of it was designated natural reserve to protect the up-land swamp ecosystem. I remember that it was difficult to do reforestation in some of these areas because of the high ground-water level. A few years after I left this position, a big power-and-heat plant was built nearby. There, as everywhere in Czechoslovakia, young brown coal was used as a fuel. From my friends who lived there, I heard that after the generating station was built, the area was often veiled in colored smoke. Another consequence was breathing difficulty for many people.

There were more negative developments; the acid ground did not need much of the resulting acid rain before the soil became so acidic that nothing could survive there. The forest dried out, first the evergreens, then the deciduous trees. I remember that we used to call a birch tree a "weed" and it was used only as a pioneer tree for reforestation of old mine sites (this district was near Jachymov, a mining area for a least six centuries). When the forest began to suffer from acid rain, the birch came into use for reforestation as the only tree which could withstand "everything." Unfortunately, that was not true. Unable to last in the acid soil, the trees deformed, stopped growing, and finally died. The soil was acidic to a depth of eighty centimetres.

Northern Erzgebirge had suffered much earlier, as a lot of industry was concentrated there and young brown coal powered the plants and factories. This coal contained sulfur and other harmful elements. The fly-ash, rich in these hazardous substances, was released directly into the atmosphere because separating or "scrubbing" devices were never installed. It was not until we came to Alberta that we saw the separation of sulfur from plant emissions. After the trees died, the water disappeared, and the swamps dried out. Invasions of insect pests were common in the now weakened forests. The Czech government used these invasions as the sole public explanation for the dying forests. Even in the early eighties, when we talked to some teachers from Erzgebirge, they still believed that the forest there was destroyed solely by insects and had no idea of the connection to acid rain.

During my last six years in Czechoslovakia, as an employee of the Environmental Department in the "land protected area," equivalent to a provincial park here in Canada, I sometimes had access to information unavailable to the public. At meetings and seminars, we heard disturbing news from experts about deteriorating ecosystems all over the country.

I will never forget my first such meeting, in 1976, in the North Bohemian mountains (in Jizerske Hory). We heard about the risk from acid rain to the whole northern part of Czechoslovakia. Before this, we knew only of the changes in the Erzgebirge mountains, but thought the rest of the forests were well and stable. Scientists from the Czech Atmospheric Research Centre showed us surprising graphs of projected atmospheric pollution which would affect all of the northern mountains. On their graphs, level three represented the worst pollution, the kind usually found close to factories, power plants, and mines; level one was the lightest level. All the mountains in northwestern, northern, and north-eastern Czechoslovakia showed as level two with some areas at level three pollution. I did not want to believe it. On our field excursions, we still saw the green forests and healthy living swamps for which these mountains were famous. However, we also saw the plumes of smoke from factories and plants in neighboring Poland and East Germany. These factories were built as close to the border as possible and the heights of Polish and East German, as well as Czech chimneys, had been recently increased, so smoke easily reached the mountains. This was the last time I saw healthy and undamaged forests in these mountains.

Three years later, on a similar field trip, we saw partly dead vegetation at the tops of mountain ridges and dried-out swamps. A new reservoir, built nearby, was unable to collect enough water, though this area had previously been a prime source of water, and was useless. Several times during these years, the International Court in the Hague, imposed large financial penalties on Czechoslovakia, Poland, and East Germany for pollution of the northern countries (Sweden, Norway, and Finland). Research showed that the source of much of Europe's pollution originated in the countries of eastern Europe but we found out only because of underground whispering, as nothing was ever published in Czech professional journals or magazines.

In 1981, I signed up for one year of postgraduate courses dealing with the environmental theme: "land use planning and conservation of natural resources." I wanted to obtain more professional knowledge in my field, but I was also attracted by student memories as the course was run by "my" university. Within the year, I heard a concentration of bad news, gloomy statistics, and cheerless prognoses about the deterioration of our environment. The future did not look bright. The researchers, professors and field workers, unable to publish their findings, were relieved when they could share these "secrets" with their students. Most of this information was horrifying.

The worst shock came in the spring when we made a field trip to northwestern Czechoslovakia, where many industries and mines were located. We learned that approximately every third child here was now born with some kind of lump, cancer, or disease. Not only was nature suffering, the pollution was affecting humans. The government dealt with the situation by paying citizens a reward, the "lasting contribution" (mockingly called the "funeral contribution") if they stayed in the area rather than moving away. Not that moving was easy. People had to apply for a permit and then wait for permission; a return to feudal practices! It was compulsory for children from this region, aged four and up, to go to month-long nature camps three or four times a year. Unfortunately, there remained fewer healthy places to go. It was said that if the children stayed continuously in the polluted areas from birth, they would die at an average age of 37 to 39 years.

We also saw the first installation of warning lights to advise the public of pollution levels. When a red light flashed in public locations, the pollution was excessive for humans and staying indoors was recommended.

The appearance of surface mining is never attractive. In north-western Czechoslovakia, brown coal is mined from the surface, even when the

- 11 -

deposits go very deep. When a mine is closed, the area is to be reclaimed. However, we saw mines which were reopened after reclamation, and which now continued to be mined for the youngest brown coal. This coal contains the highest percentage of sulfur and other harmful elements. With a composition containing three percent sulfur, it is economically sound to separate sulfur for other industrial uses, but in Czechoslovakia, sulfur is never separated, even with higher percentages of sulfur content. When brown coal is burned, everything is released into the atmosphere.

In the late seventies, the mined brown coal contained six to nine percent or more sulfur. The deposits of the youngest brown coal had even higher percentages, between 12 and 18 percent. The government originally forbade the use of this coal. However, the shortage of energy sources in Czechoslovakia changed this ruling. The government approved use of the coal, and attached no restrictions or conditions for cleaning or extraction of the harmful elements.

As a result, areas that had been reclaimed by investing a lot of money and energy, with the deepest part of the mine flooded to make a lake with grassed or forested slopes, were demolished and the mines reopened. Industry, the sector on which the government placed the most emphasis, needed more and more energy, so more coal-burning powerhouses were built. There was no chance to stop the whole destructive cycle. We were told there was no money or energy for separation devices. Even fly-ash was not filtered, or worse yet, filters were assembled and used during the working day but then the ash was puffed out during the night, so avoiding the laborious and expensive process of cleaning filters. In Prague we saw examples of the effects of these practices. As children we had eaten freely of the fruit that grew in our garden on the outskirts of the city. Now after we washed it, a deep layer of mud stayed on the bottom of the sink and if we forgot our laundry outside overnight, we had to wash it again.

The last shock came on our field excursion when we drove sixty kilometres on the road following the boundary between Czechoslovakia and East Germany. We found that this zone was covered with totally dead forests — dry trees without any life, without birds or animals. The whole area reminded me of a moon landscape or of science-fiction stories about the end of the world.

I have to confess, I was coming home from these courses deeply alarmed and stressed, and, like most of us, I did not see any solution. I absorbed only despair from all directions. At the beginning, we had made jokes and laughed at our friends from the provincial park, Jizerske Hory, saying they smelled of smoke. Two years later, we had alarming news of pollution in the other mountains: Krkonose, Orlicke Hory, Beskydy. This latter area started to dry out suddenly at all elevations above 800-900 metres. Maybe, whispered the people, the dry out was due to the escape of poisonous gas from a nearby military installation.

We still hoped our mountains would not be damaged, being far from any industrial centre. Unfortunately, new regulations allowed an increase to 300 metres for the height of factory and power plant chimneys. The damage spread, with acid pollution reaching distant locations in Czechoslovakia and the rest of Europe. While our mountains were being promoted as a first class recreational area and new plans were made for added recreational development, the local foresters were becoming aware that something was very wrong. They had tried in vain to reforest areas on windward slopes. Researchers had recommended adding lime to the soils, but the results were unremarkable because the source of the pollution remained unchecked. As the situation deteriorated, burned leaves appeared on the deciduous trees, the result of a dangerous accumulation of ozone in the air. Finally the mass dry-out of conifers occurred, first at higher elevations and on windward slopes. They lost their needles and stood bare as sad monuments to human progress.

Part of my work at the provincial park was proposal and administrative work, which led to the recognition of natural reserves within the park. One of the largest, an area between two of the highest peaks, gave me a lot of work. The original owner had proclaimed the area as a reserve in 1903. Since then it had been down-graded until now it was designated "normal productive forest." Due to its remoteness, beautiful old forest still covered the steep slopes of the high ridge but new technology threatened to make the area accessible for logging. The only way to save it was to renew the 1903 designation. My co-workers and I started the time-consuming bureaucratic process and endless administrative fights with government representatives. Now, in 1982, after nearly five years, everything was in place for the proclamation of the natural reserve.

2
The Decision

"Kdo uteče, vyhraje." — *Whoever runs away is a winner.* —
Czech proverb

In early spring 1982, I went with Petr on our annual trip to the higher
mountain elevations to hear the mating songs of the large black
grouse. Their preferred habitat was old-growth spruce forest. For us,
the closest accessible location was within the proposed natural reserve. At this time, the grouse was near extinction. Petr, who had
worked in these mountains for a long time, still remembered when he
saw five to ten males at once. In 1982, we were happy to see one bird
in the morning. To see these eight-to-ten-pound birds and hear them
sing, we had to arrive very early, still in the dark. I remember a
strange feeling as we walked through the forest, which was unusually
light. Daylight revealed the reason. On the snow beneath the trees
were high piles of needles, reminding us of heaps of hay in a stable.
The trees themselves were half dried out, with light coming through!
Some trees still had green needles in the treetops, but they were dry. A
strong wind or shaking the tree trunk made all the needles fall at once.
Our proposed natural reserve, the five years of hard work, was there,
dying, with no hope for the future. We soon found this was not the
only badly damaged place within our mountains. We made a few
more trips to the passes and mountain tops, only to see the same
picture of still green, but dry forests.

I gave in to despair. I had seen the same destruction in other places
and had heard the prognoses, but I had not really believed that the
threat from pollution was real. Suddenly, the green dry needles fell on
our heads. How could we preserve the forest or promote its growth,
when we could not stop the pollution and the destruction which
followed it. My despair and hopelessness knew no bounds. I did not
see any solution, nor did anybody else. Even the official information
talked only about the deterioration of the situation. I felt that the
threat to nature, threatened us as well. We wanted to raise our children, to have fun, and to enjoy our life and work. How could we do
these things if this threat, which we could never overcome, was
always around us. To resign ourselves to this situation, to stay, would
mean always to be afraid of what the future would bring.

In the evening, at home, we examined the situation. First we considered moving away. But where? In our country, there was hardly an undamaged area. Friends from other provincial and even national parks complained of the same problem — increasing pollution. Finally, we returned to the idea of 1968 — to flee the country. Our destination was certain from the very start: Canada.

This was our childhood dream, a spacious land with an abundance of natural beauty. Canada seemed to us a perfect country, except for the cold winter, of which we had heard. Some years later I remembered these apprehensions when I heard the group Spirit of the West sing "...We are the people of the frozen land..." How could we know how hot summers can be in the north?

There remained only one question: How to get out? We did not have many choices. Czechoslovakia is bordered on the west by Austria and West Germany. These two countries were destinations for the stream of escapees from the Eastern Bloc. Some wished to stay there, others to apply from there for emigration. To cross the border directly was almost impossible. There was barbwire netting, some of it electrified, and the entire boundary was very carefully guarded by the army. Only maniacs went directly over the wire net or people with detailed knowledge of how, where, and when to cross it. The average citizen had to find other ways to get through to the West.

It was not easy. The only possible time to apply for foreign currency was in January. Even if our friends were willing to help us obtain foreign currency, we could not go "out" as a whole family. We had to leave at least one child in Czechoslovakia. This government regulation was intended to stop the escapes which had increased to thousands per year after 1975. We immediately rejected that idea.

Yugoslavia provided our only opportunity to flee with both children. Though this country belonged to the Soviet Bloc, there were a few differences. Relations and communications with western countries were more open. Citizens of Yugoslavia had opportunities to travel to and work in western countries, an impossibility in most other socialist countries. Most importantly, the borders of Yugoslavia were guarded, but they were not blocked by barbed wire. Unfortunately, it was too late to apply for a Yugoslavian holiday on our own. There remained only one expensive option, to take a pre-paid all-inclusive vacation to Yugoslavia with Cedok, the only travel agency in Czechoslovakia. It

did not matter to us, where or when we would go for such a "trip."
We were ready to take anything and our only preference was to travel
with our own car.

Personally, I would have preferred to postpone this crossroads in our
lives. I was frightened by the suddenness of the decision as well as by
our unfamiliarity with the English language. I had learned other
languages: Russian, German, French, which I could use in a limited
way, but I had never needed the English language. However, within
one week, our nearest travel bureau confirmed the possibility of a trip
in August to Yugoslavia. The decision was made. The price of the trip?
Nearly the whole of Petr's annual wage.

Suddenly, I had the feeling that all our actions had a deadline. Everything important to us had to be finished within three months. There
was no time to procrastinate. On the other hand, we had to be careful
of every step. As escapes occurred mostly through Yugoslavia, nearly
everybody who planned a holiday there was suspect. Secrecy was
crucial. After some thought, we decided not to tell our families about
our decision. That was hard, but logical. What if they were to tell
somebody, perhaps from personal anxiety, to stop us? We both had
some family members in the communist party. Also parting from our
families would not be pleasant if they knew we might not see each
other again. Now, without this knowledge, everybody would wish us
a happy holiday.

Other problems confronted us. One collects possessions as one travels
through life. We did not cling to material things, but still, we liked
some of our treasures, especially those which were mementos or had
been hard to obtain. We knew, if our escape was successful, that the
government would automatically confiscate all our possessions. So we
decided to minimize such "voluntary gifts" and gave many things
away to our friends.

Somewhere, inside, the same question always arose: "... and what will
we do, if we don't make it?" It was our risk. We made presents of
some antiques that had been in our families for a long time. Some
things, such as Petr's two rifles, we sold. I luckily "sold" my part of
the Prague house where I grew up and which we had inherited from
my grandparents. My sister lived there and I was worried that she
would have problems with the government after our escape. I had to
find some excuse for selling because I did not want to tell her the

truth. Here the government rules helped me. It was not permitted to own two properties in Czechoslovakia at this time. I announced that we wanted to buy a house soon and for this reason I needed to sell my share of the family house. I told my sister that I needed only documentation and that she could pay me later. So that was done and, just as I had hoped, the government could not take the house from her. We were saddest about our horse. We presented it to a relative and the day he rode it away, we felt miserable. At least we decided to take our three-year-old dog, Cir, with us. He was our third generation of Hanoverian Bloodhound. Petr had owned his grandmother and father, who had lived with us until the previous year, when an elk had killed him. It would have been hard to part with Cir.

In such a mood we started to prepare the piles of possessions: one for my family, another for Petr's, and still others for friends. It became necessary to tell someone about our plans, so that they could later distribute our "gifts." Finally, we told three true friends. They were shocked and unhappy, but they helped us.

Later, even though it was difficult to be in touch with escapees, they found a way to let us know how everything had been passed on. Of course, even distributing our possessions was not easy. For their own safety, our friends couldn't admit they knew of our plan to escape. Much later, we sincerely laughed, when we read how one friend passed our gifts to my family in Prague. He actually unloaded everything in front of the house, rang the bell, hid, and observed from a distance how my horrified brother-in-law quickly moved everything inside. He was in such a hurry, when he recognized my things, that he even snatched the public mail box, which was hanging on the fence, causing the mail to fly out and scatter on the ground.

In the hamlet where we made our home, we lived in one of the two houses which had a telephone. Our neighbors and weekend residents often came by to make calls, so some explanation for the changing appearance of our living quarters had to be made. Just before our departure, we told each of our visitors that we intended to have our rooms painted while we were away, providing a logical explanation for the disappearance of our artwork, carpets, and other items. Regrettably, the antique furniture that I had inherited from my grandparents had to stay behind; to move it would have been too suspicious. We did not know that in the cities, it was common for the secret police to check the apartments of people planning holidays in Yugoslavia and western countries. Any excuse would do, to gain entry. I wonder what would have happened if someone had come to our house before we left.

In the last two weeks before our planned departure, our children, now seven and nine, went to summer camp. This gave us the opportunity we needed to clean and pack our bags more openly, as the children did not know of our intention to escape. It was difficult to chose the things that would be essential, not just for holidays but for a new life. I had a leather skirt that I had recently made and which fit me very well. I picked it up often: take it? leave it? It was not suitable for a summer holiday, so I finally left it behind. I remembered it often after our escape until I finally made a new one, here in Canada.

We needed to exchange some of our savings for foreign currency. This had to be done on the black market, with great care, as changing currency was a very suspicious act. Finally, we got some, and not unexpectedly, we needed it later in Germany.

Our biggest concern was over the anticipated border check. We had previous experience from our only prior trip to Austria, Switzerland, and West Germany. The custom officers on the Czech side checked our car so thoroughly, working for more than two hours, that they nearly took it apart on each crossing. So we knew how carefully we had to pack. We were also prepared with excuses for some things which were not exactly suited to a summer holiday, for example, we would say that we were attending the Bloodhound dog trials in Hungary, if anyone questioned Petr's hunting clothing and heavy boots. We had made such trips before, so we hoped we would be believed. Money, my jewellery, and papers such as diplomas, had to be hidden very carefully. If these things were found, it would be certain proof that we were not just going for a family holiday. My diploma, which was rolled into the car-rack, has been shaped like a cylinder ever since.

Just before our departure, our house looked as though it had been looted. Even our children, who were home for the last night, did not feel comfortable. They both carefully selected toys for our holiday: Kate chose her favorite doll, Tom a box of small cars. We had some small items out on the table, my silver bracelet and Kate's earrings, when suddenly a car pulled up in front of our house and the mayor of the nearest town came into our yard with a stranger. Petr nearly pushed me out the door in an attempt to keep the visitors outside. It turned out that the stranger was the owner of a summer house and needed my signature (I worked on the town's building committee) on a building permit, which I proceeded to sign outside, balancing the paper on my knee. After this we were too agitated to stay, so we left immediately, several hours earlier than originally planned. We even forgot the small items on our table.

3
Holiday in Yugoslavia

"What is a home? A place where we are returning. If I want to return [home] I should have freedom to leave. If I live in a place, which I cannot leave, it is not a home, it is a jail." — Jan Werich

Our first border crossing was from southern Czechoslovakia into Hungary. Border checks here were more superficial, as Hungary was also a socialist country. However, as our destination was Yugoslavia, we still expected a tough search. As we approached the border, I developed a dry mouth, my stomach was somewhere in my throat and I was unable to answer my children's questions. The line in which we had to wait only increased my nervousness. When the customs officer came to our car, we showed him our papers from the travel agency and our special grey passports, which were valid only for Yugoslavia. Our normal passports were held by the Czech police, a practice intended to deter escapees. The officer stamped our passports and indicated that we should drive out of the long line. Obediently we drove through the gate and stopped. I was sure that we would now be searched but the officer closed the gate and no-one paid any more attention to us. After a while, Petr got out of the car and asked what we were to do.

"GO!" was the answer. We could not believe our own ears. We were not even asked to open the hood after our long months of preparation, anticipation, and worry. Now we regretted all the things we had left behind because we were too scared. In the end, we had to say, "They are only things..."

We crossed Hungary peacefully, stopping for a night with friends. They told us enthusiastically of the short trips they were freely permitted to take, even to western countries. Though we said nothing, we thought about how easy it would be to go from Hungary directly to Germany.

We had another overnight stop before we reached our destination at the island of Hwar. We had just enough money to buy gas but not enough to stay overnight in a motel. As our journey covered a distance of over a thousand miles, mainly on secondary roads, we had to spend the night somewhere in the car, a common practice among visitors to Yugoslavia. The place we found showed signs of much human abuse, including all kinds of waste. As buses in most socialist countries travel nonstop, there were no public washroom facilities. The usual expression when people stop to attend to personal needs was, "Men to the right, women to the left..." It was no wonder that it was hard to find a clean place along the way.

The ferry to Hwar filled us with a holiday mood. The island itself confirmed our lighthearted feeling. Blue fields of lavender were enclosed by rock fences and slender thuas (cedars), behind which was only blue sky and sea. From the very start we had decided to enjoy our holiday, unlike some escapees, who would drive directly to a western border after crossing into Yugoslavia. We knew the crossing and the time after that could be difficult so we had decided to put aside our worries and enjoy the pleasures of our ten-day holiday.

Our accommodations were in a private house, especially built to accommodate tourists, with the landlady's own quarters in an unfinished basement. On hot days, this would be the best place to stay as the upstairs rooms were unbearably hot. Our restaurant meals were included in the tour price and that was the only place where we had contact with the tour group. The only other group activity was a boat trip to the town of Hwar. Otherwise, we were independent. Each day we tried a different beach, including one unintentional visit to a nude beach. That day we used the local boat transportation because we wanted to get near the open sea and away from the bay where we were staying. We were surprised when the guard asked for more money before the last stop, but soon found that the reason was the nude beach. This was not a problem as our children used to go naked with us to the sauna, and they liked it. The only problem was the debris and garbage on the beach.

Being in the sea most of the time, helped Tom to learn to swim and, to our surprise, even our dog, Cir, began to enjoy swimming. Previously, he had avoided water, but now he swam beyond us, far out to sea. Unfortunately, he also drank some the salt water and was sick afterwards. After that we left him with our landlady in the basement and she praised him for his obedience. We spent evenings on the promenade, watched the boats, walked through the busy market, ate ice cream or drank a glass of wine. Sometimes we bought local wine, cheese and grapes and picnicked with our children on the deck. They still remember feeling very grown up and having fun. The time passed very quickly and soon we had to pack again for the next part of our journey.

Before setting out on our holiday, I had written a letter to friends from Erzgebirge, "immigrant land," who had been permitted to move to Germany in 1967 for family reasons. I told them that we were going to Yugoslavia and would like to meet them there. Because of censorship, it was impossible to write openly, so I hoped they would understand my intentions. I proposed to meet in western Yugoslavia, at the Lublan city hall, which I hoped would be easy to find. To our surprise, we did indeed meet there at the appointed time. It was interesting, how they got my letter. Coincidentally, they had postponed their own planned holiday because Tony had experienced a severe toothache. My letter arrived the next day and, as suddenly as it had started, the toothache stopped. They did not need to visit the dentist and went to Yugoslavia rather than holidaying in Italy, as they had originally planned. On the day of our meeting, they were waiting nervously for us. They knew exactly what we had in mind.

We assessed our situation, not a bright one with our grey passports. Even to enter Hungary, we had needed additional documents. Our plan was to cross the border into Austria and drive through to West Germany, where we would apply for emigration to Canada. We believed that our waiting period in Germany would be more bearable than elsewhere, as we had friends living there. We also believed the whisper network back in Czechoslovakia, which said the process of application to other countries went faster in Germany than in Austria. Later, we found, it was just the opposite. We had one further objection to staying in Austria. Just before we had left for our holiday, two Czechs had been officially returned from Vienna. Nobody knew why, but the Czech government pressed the advantage gained by this precedent and stated publicly that the Austrian government would be returning all escapees to Czechoslovakia.

We decided to chance crossing the border. Our friends would have no difficulties so they could either precede or follow us. We would decide on the next step later.

4
Crossing the Borders

"Most men have more courage than even they themselves think they have." — Lord Greville

And so we started.

Surely enough, they turned us back to Yugoslavia right away because of our passports. Neither our excuses nor pleading, such as: "We would like to see Austria just for one day..." or "We have an invitation to a wedding..."(which, thanks to our other friend, we really had) mattered. When we returned to Yugoslavia, we said to our children, that we would like to visit our German friends, who we just met, but we don't have the proper papers. We did not mention escaping because if we didn't succeed it would be easier for all of us. The children happily welcomed the new adventure. From the start, they liked our friends, Anita and Tony, and they wanted to visit them.

We tried the other crossing with the same result. They sent us back. We even tried crossing into Italy. The young officer told us quietly, if it was a weekday and evening, we would have more of a chance. But it was Saturday, and on the weekends he worked with another guard, a member of the communist party, who was specially selected to protect the border. However, our nerves were too strained to wait until the next week. Not far away there was one more crossing. We decided to use a method, advised among friends in Czechoslovakia: we put some German money with the passport and waited to see how that would work. It was a disaster! The customs officer began to shout, what did we think, how dare we try to corrupt the officers, he knew our kind and our dangerous intentions, and so on. Finally, he took Petr into the office, to write a report with him. As well, he ordered us to report in Prague within the next twenty-four hours. So the final decision was made for us. Any kind of report about illegal intention to cross the border to the West would ruin our lives. We had heard about people who were sentenced just for suspicion of intent to defect. They usually lost their jobs and found only manual labor, were not allowed to travel, and their children had no access to higher education, such as college or university.

On our return from the border, we again met our friends, who had crossed the line back and forth many times that day. It seemed that our only chance was to leave the car in Yugoslavia and walk across the border somewhere away from the customs offices. We would meet our friends again on the other side, cross Austria together, and then cross the border to Germany. We talked about it at our late lunch in the town of Planica, which we knew previously as the location of the world championship in ski jumping. But this afternoon, we were so nervous, we could not enjoy this pleasant place nor the delicious food. Only our children were content and enjoyed the lunch. Afterwards, we drove to a remote parking lot and transferred everything we could, from our carefully selected belongings, to Tony's car. We would keep with us only one bag and the children's toys, in case our friends were searched.

All of us, including the dog, squeezed into Tony's car. About two kilometres from the border crossing was a turnoff to a forest road, noticed on our first, unsuccessful, attempt to cross. Here, our family left the car. We wished each other "Good luck," and set off. After a while, we turned right through the bush and according to our estimate of the proper direction, went straight to freedom. The terrain was similar to the foothills: rolling ground, where the hills and knolls alternated with ravines and depressions. All was covered by bushes and shrubs.

Kate cheerfully marched with Petr and Cir, but Tom was falling behind and I had to drag him along. Petr and Kate sat on a knoll and while waiting for us, Petr looked around with his binoculars. All around him the terrain had been cleared of underbrush and directly below was a watch house. It was actually a watch-line around the border crossing! How quickly we ran from there! Suddenly, after fighting through dense bush, we came to a different kind of forest. It was much easier to walk through the older trees with minimum underbrush. As we heard the traffic noise from the highway, we knew we were getting close to it. Petr went carefully to check where to go. How happy we were when he found our friends' car parked only a few metres away. We had made it to Austria! At the same moment we heard the alarm whistling from the border guards. I don't need to say how fast we jumped into the car and drove off without waiting to find the reason for the alarm. The next summer, at the same border crossing, the guards shot two escapees.

We drove through Austria without stopping, happy that this part of our journey was behind us. Ahead of us lay the border crossing to Germany. Anita and Tony assured us, that should not be a problem. Our previous experience was that German customs officers usually did not ask for documents and if they ever did, only for the driver. But we had bad luck. At the time, police were looking for some kidnappers from Italy and Yugoslavia, who were selling children in West Germany. The officer at the Salzburg border crossing looked into our car and saw the children, in their shorts and shirts, asleep after their long bush walk. He immediately asked to whom the children belonged and wanted to see our documents. This was a major problem with our invalid passport and no visas. On top of it all, this time our problem could threaten our friends. The flow to West Germany had already flooded the refugee offices. In an attempt to reduce the number of escapees, the government had increased the penalty to their own citizens who gave help to refugees. Petr and I did not know at the time that our friends were now at risk.

The customs officer directed us to the police station. Petr and Tony quickly put together a "story" about how we met in Yugoslavia. We would say that we had car trouble, which we were unable to fix. We were going to West Germany to buy a new part and would then return to Yugoslavia to repair our car. The older officer, who was wearing a hat with a big feather, listened skeptically. Finally, he asked if we intended to apply for refugee status. In a flash, everything flew through our heads: "It would be easy, but we did not want to give our friends trouble. And what about returning escapees?..." So we stuck with our story, that we only wanted to go for a car part to West Germany.

"In this case," said the officer, "it is impossible without a valid passport and proper visa. You have to stay in Austria until Monday." (This was Saturday evening.) "Go to the police station, they will check your papers and decide your status."

We were in despair, but we couldn't change the decision. The policemen helped us to find a cheap room in a small hotel. Of course, we had to pay for it ourselves. Our friends had to leave. They took some of our belongings and also our dog, as he would now be only a burden to us. So Cir was the first successful immigrant from our family.

As we were staying just a short distance away, we went to Salzburg on Sunday. I had good memories of this beautiful historic city in the foothills of the Alps. The narrow streets remain as they were in Mozart's time. I had liked the small shops which sold wood-carvings — especially those made from the beautiful sweet-smelling Limba Pine, the markets with booths offering salt pretzels, chocolates, and "Mozart's candy." The coffee houses, candy and baker's shops, as well as restaurants had outside tables so that visitors could enjoy the panorama of the Alps. The Alps held a special attraction for me, and I had visited Salzburg and its castle, which is located on a hill above the city, twice previously and had greatly enjoyed the views. Today, the weather was hot and we were nervous due to the uncertainty of our position here, though I recalled my previous visits, the first with my brother, the second with Petr. On that last occasion, we had a two-day permit to travel to a dog exhibition in Vienna, and had driven home through Salzburg, just to glance at the Alps. Now, preoccupied as we were, we found ourselves unable to enjoy the beauty of the setting or the many small shops of this historic place. Our only wish was to be far away! Disappointed, we returned to our hotel to find we had a visitor, Tony.

He had not wanted to leave us here alone and we were very thankful for it. We were unable to plan ahead, as we did not know what the Austrian police intended to do with us. However, Tony had already scouted the area around the Austrian-German border and gave us hope. We could easily walk through.

That evening, we told our children the truth, that we would like to go to Canada and not return to Czechoslovakia. In the small hotel room, suited maybe for newlyweds but not for four members of a very nervous family, our children started to perceive our steps to a different life. Their first response was joy and the thrill of sudden adventure. But immediately after, there came feelings of sadness over their loss. They remembered their family and friends, "Will we see them again?" and the toys they left behind. We had to talk to them as with adults, and explain our reasons and feelings to lessen their uneasiness. "Toys can be bought and we will gain healthy, unspoiled nature and the feeling of freedom and honor." We told them, "We will find new friends and keep in touch with our good friends and families." After a while, a cheerful mood toward the future prevailed in our children. Unfortunately, Petr and I couldn't join them — we felt worried about the insecurity of the next hours and events.

Monday morning, with a feeling of doom, we reported to the police station in Salzburg. Tony was already there. They questioned us, wrote out our "fairy tale," stamped it, let us sign it, and then brought in the sentence. Because we had infringed on Austrian law, we would be sent immediately to Czechoslovakia under police supervision. As we did not have a car, the police would take us to the railroad station and watch our departure to our country of origin. It looked very bad for us. Tony, who so far had acted only as a "witness" began to bargain, "Look, if you send them home with police documents, they will have terrible problems. What if I take them to the railroad station myself and buy them tickets? They will have enough problems to explain when they return through Austria instead of Hungary. Without police assistance, it will be much easier. I myself guarantee, they will leave Austria today." The last words were exactly what the Austrian police wanted to hear. So they agreed.

Again, with great relief, we found ourselves in Tony's car. We did not talk much, but we knew Tony was not driving to the city centre and the railroad station, but in the opposite direction, out of the city, west to the German boundary. Not far from the hotel where we had spent the two previous nights, we got out. We determined the direction to go and made our arrangements with Tony. In two hours, he would drive slowly on the German side of the highway, some clothing fluttering from his car window, so we would easily recognize his car.

We set off on our march. This time, the terrain was different. There was mostly farmland, with only islands of forest, near the Austrian-German boundary. There were also strips of swamp that were impossible to cross, as we soon found out. We tried to keep the highway in sight and had to take care not be seen. From time to time we encountered the swamps and had to walk around them. Later, we learned that these swamps posed insurmountable obstacles for many people.

If I was nervous before, how could I describe it now? I realized how important it was to cross the boundary without any further trouble. For us, there was no way back. My tongue, due to hot weather and stress, was stuck to my palate, my knees were weak, but we had to walk fast. Above all, I knew I had to be a model and support for our children. Finally, we came to a mature deciduous forest. Walking here was easy and we even found a good path. The highway roared, very close. We also smelled water. In a while, we found out why. Suddenly, we came to a river. Not a creek, a river. It was about fifty metres wide and visibly deep. We could not believe it, Tony had not mentioned any water. The highway was above us on the bridge. We followed the river in both directions, but found no other bridge. I am a good swimmer, but I could not risk swimming across with our children. The worst of it was that we did not know whether we were still in Austria or already in Germany. Finally, we decided that the only thing to do was to cross the river on the highway bridge.

Imagine how conspicuous every pedestrian is on a highway bridge. Now imagine a whole family. We were somewhere in the middle of the bridge, when a car stopped in front of us. A civilian stepped out, pulled a police hat from the back of the car, and with a smile waited for us. However, our feeling was far from a smile as we did not yet know if the policeman was from Austria or Germany. Until now, all translation had been done by Tony. Presently, it was my turn. This moment was very decisive for us, but this feeling did not help me in my concentration. To the policeman's smiling question, "So where are you heading?" I should probably have answered something cheerful. Instead, I nearly shouted, "Where are we, in Germany or Austria?" I guess you could hear the stone fall from our hearts when we heard the answer, "In Germany, the customs house is over there, on the hill." It was about 600-700 metres from us!

With this important information, I confessed right away, "We would like to apply for refugee status, but actually we would like to go to Canada." We must have appeared funny, standing there in t-shirts and running shoes, with two little dirty children, only one bag and Kate's doll, explaining that we would like to go to Canada. I do not know what the policeman thought about us, but he directed us into the car, turned back and drove to the customs house.

I was alarmed, "No, we don't want to go to Austria. Please, we want to stay in Germany. You cannot do it, please, don't take us to Austria!" It took time to explain that he was only a highway patrolman, so he needed to find other police, who would take us to the police station. From the customs house, he would be able to call, and we had to wait there. This explanation lessened my nervousness just slightly. The customs house was only a small building with two rooms, one for Austrian and one for German customs officers. The hall between the two was tiny, and we a hard time to fit into it. There we were, actually one step from Austria, from which we had been banished that same morning. I had butterflies in my stomach and could hardly talk. I started to feel better when the other policeman came, in full uniform. After another hour of waiting, we found ourselves again on the highway, this time in Germany.

We did not drive far. We stopped at a police station in a small town located in the foothills of the Alps. There the children and I were separated from Petr so that we could not talk together during questioning. The police said my German language was good enough that I did not need a translator. However, I later found out that Petr was not so lucky. He was put in jail to wait for a translator, definitely a new experience.

My examination lasted about two hours, uninterrupted, except when Tom became bored and made "mirror shine" with his metal box, directly in the policeman's face. The officer tried to overlook it, but after a while he sternly warned both of us. He questioned me about our life in Czechoslovakia, our reason for escaping, and how we made it. Here I had a problem. I wanted to tell the truth but did not want to mention the help of our friends. When he asked how we travelled through Austria, I did not not answer clearly, but when the policeman repeated the question and suggested somebody's help, I said "No." Right away, he lost his calm face and said he would leave the question open in case I changed my mind.

After a while, he left the room and I suddenly heard, from next door, among other voices, the familiar voice of Tony. When the policeman came back, he started to explain that if we wanted to apply for refugee status in Germany, we had to tell them the truth. I concluded that they had probably found Tony and he had admitted helping us.

Later I learned that I was right. Tony probably appeared too suspicious when he slowly drove several times along the same section of highway near the border, with clothing fluttering through the window. Tony did not dare to tell lies and all our stories had to be the same. If not, the small police station would not commit to a decision about us. Of course, we learned all this later. When I realized that Tony was at the station, I told the truth and saw how relieved the policeman looked. He even suggested that my answer was different because I did not previously understand the question.

Petr tried to deny our story for the longest amount of time. His questioner even started to shout at him. Finally the translator helped Petr with a quiet remark that he was sure that the policeman knew the truth so it would be better to say so openly. Petr confessed the help of our friends, and then all three protocols were equal. When we signed the statements, it was a relief not only for us but also for the police. Suddenly, they lost their official faces and when our family was reunited, they happily wished us all the best and nice stay in Germany while waiting for Canada.

It was after nine in the evening. The children were hungry and tired and we adults were worn out from the stress of the day's events. Our escorting policeman explained that he was taking us out for supper and afterwards to some accommodations. We did not see any more of Tony that evening. The late supper was in a restaurant owned by a man from Yugoslavia. He gave us beer with our meal, for welcome, and said "Everything is paid." He knew some Czech words and stressed that we would be surprised at the number of people from Czechoslovakia here. After we had eaten, we were driven a short distance to a pension (similar to a bed and breakfast) where the elderly landlady was already preparing a room for us on the second floor. We put clean sheets on the beds, washed and went to bed. We did not know what we would do the next day or if we would be moved again. However, we were thankful for the quiet night.

5
Aufham

"Unser Dorf soll schöner werden." — Our village should be always more beautiful. — motto of Aufham

Following directions given by our landlady, we arrived in the morning at a coffee room for breakfast. We were surprised to see that breakfast was being served as if for guests, with trays of coffee pots, milk, freshly baked buns, butter and jam. But the biggest surprise was the nationality of the other people in the room. All of them were Czechs. The pension had six rooms and five of them were already occupied by escapees. The sixth would be taken that evening, when the local police delivered another family with two childen. All the rooms filled up in three days. The same scenario was being enacted all over Aufham, the village in which we were staying.

German immigration law stated that escapees had to stay in the location where they were originally detained until their landed immigrant status was granted. The area near Salzburg was the location of one of the busiest passes between Austria and Germany. Many people, like ourselves, managed to cross Austria and either turned themselves in or were detained at the German border. This year the police were dealing with growing numbers of escapees. Hotels and bed-and-breakfast operations designated for refugees were operating beyond capacity. The government had to hastily find more and more new accommodation. As we later learned, the German government paid well for providing room and board to refugees. Many innkeepers preferred a sure profit from refugees, even with some risk, to the uncertainty of catering to tourists, especially now, in September, when the main season was over. In the case of our own landlady, refugees were very profitable. Her furnishings were not up to the usual standards, so she did not have the chance of many German guests. Now all her rooms, including an attic room, were full — with three family groups, one unmarried couple and two young men. The landlady was very strict about regulations: breakfast was at 8:00 o'clock, we could bathe once a week, we were expected to clean and were permitted to wash one load of laundry per week. For lunches and suppers we went to the "Yugoslavian" restaurant. However, mostly good cheer and humor prevailed, despite the occasional problem arising from this gathering of unique people thrown together by circumstance.

The next day, we found, we were actually free to do mostly as we pleased. We had some duties: a visit to the nearest town to report at an immigation office, and some official papers to complete regarding our stay; otherwise, the days were our own. Though we were tied to a single area by our accommodation and board arrangements, it was like a beautiful holiday to be in this tiny Bavarian village in the foothills of the Alps. It was even more like a holiday when we compared it to our recent stay in Yugoslavia because then we were subconsciously fearful of the future, of how we would manage the border crossing, and the difference between the two worlds. These feelings were common to all the escapees as we had all experienced much the same dramatic journey. Suddenly, it was over. All the months of preparation and planning were behind us and we walked freely on the other side of the "iron curtain." It reminded me of what I had read about the 1896-98 Klondike Goldrush: that most of the people who arrived at their destination, having crossed the harsh terrain, lost their interest in gold mining. They just poured over the streets of Dawson City, happy and content that they had managed the difficult journey, unwilling to expend any more energy on other ventures. It was not quite this traumatic for us. We still had energy, but we remember the first days of our stay in Germany as a beautiful time to soothe our nerves.

Everyone lived these first days according to their inclination. Our family engaged in such activities as short walks around our village, swimming in the local outdoor pool, and browsing through shops in the village or in the nearby town. It was no secret that the economies of the Eastern Bloc were stagnant under the communists. Before WWII Czechoslovakia was the third most developed European country. Now the incompetence of the communist leadership placed us at the low end of the development scale. One result was a limited market for nearly all commodities. There was a shortage of necessities, such as food, as well as of luxury products, like cars. To obtain consumer goods, we had to stand in lines, to constantly investigate sources of supply for goods, and to rely on the help of friends and relatives to find and obtain needed items. Suddenly, here in Germany, the situation was quite different. We looked on displays of many kinds of goods which were, simply, available. Nobody had to search for them or stand in line. Unfortunately, we lacked the money to buy. Even the smallest shop in Aufham was equal to the best Czech shops, TUZEX, the privilege shops, where one had to pay by special vouchers which could be obtained in exchange for foreign currency.

No wonder that, during our first days in Germany, we could not resist browsing through the shops, not to buy, but just from curiosity. However, unlike some of the refugees who spent day after day in the shops, even with no money, Petr, the children, and I preferred wandering around Aufham. To the others, we probably seemed odd when we showed our enthusiasm for pleasures other than consumer goods. Above all, we were amazed by the air and water quality. A creek running through the middle of the village had trout in it. This seemed very unusual to us, as we could not remember seeing any fish in Czech village creeks. The springs and brooks around Aufham were so clear that we could drink from them.

The forest here consisted of beech, spruce, and fir. The fall crop of beechnuts was enormous. We took many trips just to collect bags full of the seeds, which we then peeled to enjoy the nutty flavour. Back in Czechoslovakia, the first trees to die due to acid rain were firs, a result of their greater sensitivity to pollution. The beeches lost their reproductive ability and young seedlings became hard to obtain. For a while, they were imported from Slovakia to the Czech Republic, but the shipments had recently stopped as Slovakia also experienced a shortage of seeds. Now, not so far from Czechoslovakia, we saw forests which continued to thrive despite centuries of human agricultural activity occurring around them. When we talked about this in the evenings with our friends back at the hotel, many of them were surprised how spoiled the environment of their homeland had been.

As we were so close to the mountains, we tried to fulfill our dream to hike in the Alps. In the first week, we made a trip to the highest peak in the area, Hochistaufens, 1772 metres high, which was accessible directly from our village. The children went with us, and although it was a long and difficult walk, they were happy scrambling on the steep rocky path.

I remember participating in a lot of discussions in the first days. In Aufham we met people from all the countries of the Eastern Bloc, though Czechs and Slovaks predominated. Everybody was keen to tell their story, so when the children had been put to bed, we met with the other adults in the hallway, which became our "social club." Unfortunately, we did not have access to the coffee room except at breakfast.

Sometimes we bought a bottle of the cheapest wine and salted peanuts — then we talked. Probably this was a response to the months of enforced silence, when we had to take care that our plans for escape did not become known. Now we listened to the stories of others and talked about our own "adventure," comparing what we should have done and what could have happened, if we had acted in another way. ... And more and more, we started to talk about our future. Over all, it was a beautiful holiday. What more could one ask: beautiful setting, adequate accommodation and food, and the good company of others, who shared our feelings and with whom we had fun.

Unfortunately, within a couple of weeks, our holiday feelings faded away as new problems arose. The worst disappointment for us was the news from a Czech-Canadian agency in Munich, which arranged emigration to Canada from Germany. When we finally were able to contact them, they told us that each year, the Canadian government accepts only a certain number of refugees from Germany, and that this quota was filled. We had to wait until next year. We were told that our application had to be in the office on January 1st but not before in order to be considered. The quota for 1982 was 300 people, not families — people! This was a very small amount compared with the thousands of emigrants, arriving each year in West Germany. We tried to make other connections in the meantime, to find addresses of friends living in Canada, but we had a foreboding — our stay in Germany would be longer than we had first thought.

Our friends Anita and Tony came to visit us during those first days in Aufham. We discussed with Tony, over and over, our crossing of the border and the police examinations. Tony was worried about the impact it would have on him. He did not have to wait long to find out. A few months later he had a court date and was sentenced to pay a fine of 1 500DM ($750 Canadian) plus court expenses. The only money we had was exactly 1 500DM as we had been unable to exchange more before we departed from Czechoslovakia. So we paid the fine, and Tony the expenses. We were glad Anita and Tony did not hold it against us, and we stayed friends. Actually, their main concern was that Tony could lose his job. Fortunately, this did not happen.

Anita and Tony still had our dog, Cir, in their apartment in Bad Tolz, 150 km away. Now we ran into a problem. Our landlady absolutely refused to take Cir in the hotel, even when we offered to pay extra and to keep him in the yard. Anita and Tony's family loved Cir and he was enjoying being with them. However, we knew that as a working dog, used to being outside, the idle life in town was not good for him. Also, we did not want to take advantage of our friends. We had to find another solution.

Then an order came that our children had to start school. We were surprised. Until now, nobody had thought about school in Germany. We had Canada on our minds, and had begun to prepare for intensive learning of English. Now, that was out of the question, as the children had to start German school and, of course, they did not know the language. From our first day here, I had often helped with translation as very few of the refugees knew German. Now with the additional task of helping the children to learn German, my own study of English had to be postponed. Tom started grade two, Kate grade four. The other children in our hotel were placed in grades ranging from one to three. At this time, alarming stories were circulating of how sometimes the children of escapees were kidnapped and sent back to their original country so that their parents would be forced to return. Even if we convinced each other that we were not so important that it could happen to us, we were forced to accompany our children every morning, noon and afternoon, to and from school. Three couples from our hotel rotated the responsibility of the daily walks with the children, the duty parent resembling a hen with chicks covering the several blocks to the school.

It is amazing, how fast children are able to learn another language. Within two months, they were competent to communicate and joined the regular class in their work. Unfortunately, there was no time to teach them English until the next holiday. Even for myself, it was not a good environment for learning English as I had to use and work on my own German language skills first.

In the meantime, our stay became less comfortable. German law ensured us free accommodation and board during the time we were waiting for landed immigrant status, which was called "Azyl" in German. Unfortunately, even if we did not want to stay in Germany, we had to first obtain the "Azyl" status. During the waiting period, we did not have a permit to work and had to stay in the accommodation arranged for us by the government. Some people knew of this provision ahead of time, but some, including ourselves, did not have any idea of what to expect. So our hope of making some money before we would go to Canada was in vain. I could not judge how well this arrangement worked for the German government. It was definitely very expensive, and from our point of view, it did not have any logic. I would have preferred to work, pay our own expenses, and have a feeling of usefulness and the right to make our own decisions. In this way of living, we had to take what we got, without other choices. We could buy hardly anything as we lacked money. Later, families with children were given a small allowance, $10 per month, so we could at least buy some fruit.

The food was often not good and the menu was repeated monotonously every week. Kate disliked fish for many years due to the sole which we got each Friday in the form of a hard, dry roasted meal accompanied with sour potato salad. We did not get sufficient fruit, fresh vegetables, or milk for the children. It was necessary to buy some food and that meant making some money, even without a permit.

I saw that the small restaurants and hotels did not take the prohibition to employ refugees too seriously, but the summer season was over, and many businesses were closing. However, we were lucky. Petr has been interested in carving since childhood. He carves antlers and bones, mostly jewelry pieces: brooches, bracelets, pendants, belt buckles and even letter openers. With time, he also learned to carve wood, mostly to touch up rifle stocks. His work appealed to visiting hunters. Here in Bavaria, we were in a location where carving is an honored tradition. Any products made from antler were in great demand and carved jewelry was part of the national costume. To tell the truth, we had hoped and counted on the chance to make some money by selling Petr's carvings.

Petr doesn't need many tools for his work. He had brought from home the curved chisels and the small saw needed to work with antlers. The blades had always been imported from Germany. The only tool, which we did not dare to take with us, was a dentists' laboratory drill, which Petr used for finishing work. My father used to say that Petr uses a drill to give life to animals which he has carved. Definitely, Petr needed this tool for his carving and we were very happy when some friends helped us.

From the time when I finished university, I have been in touch with a friend who escaped to Switzerland, with his girlfriend, in 1968. Petr and I had visited with them on one other occasion and they were, by this time, married with two boys. His wife, now a dentist, had just started to furnish her own office.They were among the first people that we called when we had successfully emigrated. They were very surprised as they had thought we were in jail somewhere, for the letter I had sent them before our holiday had shown our intention to escape all too clearly. They drove the 600 km to visit us the next weekend and brought with them the drill Petr needed. We are still grateful for this. All the friendship shown to us at this time provided strong psychological support, and in this case, also economic aid. The drill was very helpful in making money that would get us to Canada.

Petr worked from our hotel room at first. He did not need much space, but carving makes a very fine dust, so I had to clean the room several times a day. A bigger problem was the drilling, as it makes noise and takes electric power. Our landlady was especially concerned about the use of electricity so we had to be very careful. We were fortunate to meet the village mayor soon after Petr had started this work and we asked him for advice about finding a work space. He was very helpful and arranged for a room, used by craft and music groups, in a public recreation building. The mayor wrote Petr's reservation in the schedule as "craft-carving" giving him access to space in the building. As well, when we were talking, we mentioned the problem with our dog to the mayor. He recommended that we visit a local professional hunter.

This professional hunter was a government employee, similar to a fish and wildlife officer, except that he was employed by the forestry office and worked mainly in the field. In winter, he was responsible for game, which included feeding, and in summer, he was responsible for the hay crop and maintenance of facilities such as cabins and feeding stations. In the fall, he worked as a guide. We were told that this professional hunter's dog, the same breed as our dog, had died in the spring. With hope in our hearts, we made a visit to him.

Generally, village residents did not trust the refugees, though no particular problem or conflict had occurred so far. However, there was a difference between people who had lived in this place generation after generation and the current wave of immigrants. They saw us doing nothing, and knew we were supported through their taxes. Unemployment was a problem in Germany, as everywhere in the West, and often the media pointed out how immigrants and foreign workers were taking over jobs. The greatest intolerance was against workers from Yugoslavia and Turkey, who were willing to work for the lowest wages. In reality, they took mostly positions for which no German would apply. However, the distrust and even hate prevailed, and little distinction was made between emigrants from different countries.

Our first visit to the hunter's family was definitely influenced by this common feeling. However, Kurt, after a bit of hesitation, agreed to try our dog for a while. He was to get a puppy within a month, so he wanted to return Cir to us then. Petr mentioned that a puppy is easier to raise with an adult dog, but we did not push the matter. We just hoped that when Kurt and his family had a chance to know and work with our dog for a while, they would not return him so easily. Cir was a young dog, but very well trained, calm, and obedient. He was used to being mostly outdoors, but behaved well, even in a house. If we told him to stay in a place, in a home or out in the field, he would stay — even for a whole day. When Anita and Tony brought Cir from the city, he was as big as a small pig. Each member of their family had liked and spoiled him and found that parting from him was hard. It was time for Cir to change host families again, and we hoped that all would go well for him.

As I mentioned, Kurt worked mostly in the field. His district was about twenty kilometres from Aufham. Especially now, in the fall, with hunting guests arriving, Kurt was in need of a good bloodhound. In Germany, as in most of Europe, it is the law that hunters must find any game they wound and must use a well-trained dog for this purpose. Bloodhounds are specially trained for tracking wounded game animals. Due to their sensitive noses, these dogs are able to find tracks which can be many hours, even three days, old and follow them for a long time. Training a bloodhound is a long complicated process and it is impossible to make a good tracker within a single season. There are two kinds of bloodhounds in Europe: Hanoverian — like Cir, and Bavarian, a smaller breed. The North American bloodhound is only a distant relative of these two. The Hanoverian is one of the oldest breeds in Europe and is in high regard for this type of work. Petr and I have bred and worked with bloodhounds since we finished forestry studies. Petr, especially, has a lot of experience. Unfortunately, there are not many good dogs, so we had to exchange internationally within Europe for breeding stock. Breeding dogs are selected from those that have the best results at exhibitions and exams held throughout Europe. These trials were also a place where we came to meet and know many new friends.

As we had hoped, the longer Cir stayed with Kurt's family the more content they became. Kurt prized him for his obedience and how Cir calmly waited for him, not only in the field but also in the car, when Kurt had to do some office work. Cir eventually accompanied Kurt everywhere, because Kurt felt comfortable with him. Resi, Kurt's wife also prized Cir for his quiet behavior at home and his appetite for all he was given. At their home, he would come to be petted, but never annoyed anybody and mostly stayed in his own place.

After three weeks, when Kurt got a puppy, there was no more talk about returning Cir to us. It is true that a puppy learns faster with an older dog. The young Bavarian bitch was full of energy and "wild," as Resi used to say. However, after two months, she followed Kurt with Cir "at heel." Unfortunately, at home she still ran wild, much to Resi's affliction. She, therefore, prized Cir even more.

Simply put, Cir had a beautiful year. He was very useful at finding game, though this was his last opportunity to work this way, as he had no chance to do any tracking in Canada. We were also lucky to have met Kurt and his family. We gradually made friends with them and have kept in touch ever since. As our friends, they made our stay in Germany not only more bearable, but memorable.

Here I should tell about a discussion with our friends, Kurt and Resi, who helped me to understand something new about World War II. Within the communist regime, we thought that all Germans believed in and supported Hitler's goverment. However, here in Bavaria, we found that nearly all Bavarians had hated him, if for nothing else, then because Hilter was against religion and Bavarians generally held strong Catholic beliefs. Yet, the story of Resi's father is unusual. As nearly every German male, his father had to join the army, even though he was personally strongly against the war. After a while, he managed to desert, and for this he would pay with his life if he were caught. He went home to the family farm — where else? Only his wife knew he was there and she helped him to hide in the barn, in the straw. There he stayed, for nearly two years without anybody else knowing, including their children. Only in this way, he had a chance to survive and not be found by the Gestapo, when they came from time to time to look and ask for him. There, in the barn, he lived to finally see the end of the war, when he could again work on his farm — ordinary but brave people.

Because of Cir, we had more opportunities to get away from our accommodations than other refugees. According to the regulations, we could only leave our hotel if someone signed for us. We were able to visit Anita and Tony's home several times when we needed to go to the Canadian refugee office in Munich, as they lived not far from it. Our other friends invited us to dog shows and exams, which took us even further from our home base. Our main problem was transportation, as we always needed a ride, not having our own car. Friends were able to help with this problem and thanks to one such trip, we met another family, who were later a lot of help to us.

At one bloodhound fanciers' meeting, Cir made the top exam. He was the only one of several dogs who made it, finding a wild boar in the hunting grounds of a German nobleman. The smell of wild boar is unpleasant to dogs and they don't like to track them. This one was shot and wounded a day before the exam and 25-30 cm of snow fell over-night. Petr started to work with Cir on the track the next day around noon. Cir masterfully checked the marked tracks, steadily stretched his leash, and led Petr down an invisible trail. He stopped at each drop of blood, since buried under snow. In the thickest part of the forest, he stepped several paces aside from the tracks and found an antler. It was one from the biggest elk, and foresters had been looking for it since spring. Cir did not delay, continued on the boar's trail, and coming to a small clearing, pointed to a heap of snow. It would have been easily overlooked in the rough terrain, but it was indeed the dead wild boar. It had not taken long; the boar had travelled only one kilometre, but with the fresh snow and the nature of the terrain, there was no hope of finding it without a good dog. The happy nobleman gave Petr the antler, and Petr already knew what he would do with it.

After such trips, Kurt's family waited for our visits eagerly and delighted in listening to our stories. We also saw that Cir was happy to return to his host family. Once Petr's pride in his well-trained dog received a shock. Kurt had invited us to visit his cabins and then hike with him in his hunting area. Cir, who as usual, went along without a leash, did not follow Petr but Kurt. I have to explain that our dog had his priorities. If our whole family went out, he followed Petr. If it was only myself and the children, he followed me. Kurt was master in this location, Cir his daily companion here, and above all, Kurt had the gun. So Cir abandoned Petr and followed Kurt.

We became good friends with Kurt's family, and as they lived close by, we could stop there in the afternoons or evenings for short visits. Later, we spent some weekends or holidays in the cabins near Aufham or at Kurt's hunting grounds. In Bayern, the children had many religious holidays throughout the school year and to be away from the hotel was a welcome change for the family. We were well satisfied with our solution to the "dog problem."

Government housing — our last home in Czechoslovakia.

Camping with our horse.

Driving to
Yugoslavia.

Swimming in
Yugoslavia.

Aufham, our first accommodation in Germany.

Tom, on top of Hochstaufens by Aufham.

By Königsee, St. Bartoloma's Church in the background.

Coffee with the hunter's family.

6
Moving to Königsee

"I feel anxious and regret that I have to leave [nature] and spend time among people, many people..." — Jan Smid

Our pleasant stay in Aufham was marred only by the occasional problem with our landlady. As winter drew near, we began to resent the minimal heating and having to take warm showers. At home we always used to shower more than once a week, and with hot water. Here we had only lukewarm water, because the landlady refused to set the water heater any higher. From October onward, we wore additional sweaters in our rooms as the room temperature never went above 16 degrees Celsius. The family living in the attic room found a mobile power heater in the adjacent storage room. So we secretly moved it from room to room to slightly warm our chilly accommodations. We had to be on guard in the hallway, so the landlady would not discover us. Many times, we had to rush back to the attic carrying the still hot heater. Our evening meetings in the hallway continued, with the participants wrapped in blankets, drinking tea or cheap hot wine to give the illusion of warmth. We did not have permission to cook anything but our electric kettle was always in use. In the mornings, we heated milk for the children as the scheduled breakfast was served after they had gone to school.

As we compared the stories of the refugees from our hotel and from the rest of the village, we found that only a few with visas had found their way directly to West Germany. Most of the escapees had taken a holiday to Yugoslavia, as we had, and, with more or less luck, had made the crossing to the West. Some had obtained a visa in Yugoslavia for travelling through Austria, or even West Germany, on their way back to Czechoslovakia. We had been unaware of this opportunity. However, we were not the only ones with a complicated escape. One young refugee was caught by German police as he pretended to be doing an orientation race. He carried only a small bag and a big bib with a number. Another young man, a skilled gardener, was sure that he was saved by his pruners. He apparently was trapped somewhere close to the boundary among a tangle of blackberries, and was able to cut his way out with pruning shears. It sounded as if he was in a fairy tale, seeking a princess. Here the princess had a name, Liberty.

Two families had decided to separate so their escape would be easier. In one case, an expectant mother went to visit her relatives in Germany while her husband and small daughter went to Yugoslavia. From there they set out on foot for Germany. He crossed the boundary in nearly the same place as we did. Between Austria and Germany, he staggered unaware into the swamp meadows as he was travelling at night. With a child on his shoulders, a bag in his hand and knee deep in water, he was in despair, not knowing what to do next. Luckily for him, the boundary patrol sighted him from the road. Even after all this time, he kept repeating to us how glad he was when they had helped him. And on top of that, how glad he was to find he was already in Germany where his wife was nervously waiting for them. In the case of the second family, the mother and two children went to Yugoslavia while the husband went with his friend to Germany. There, he rented a German car and drove to Yugoslavia to pick up the rest of his family. Of course, he was taking the risk that nobody would check him too carefully at the border crossings. His wife and children were travelling with a tour group, so it was not as easy for them to leave as it had been for us. They had to meet secretly and were worried that their children would openly show their happiness about their father's arrival. They finally made their departure, safely crossed Austria, but were stopped at the German border. However, as the husband had a German visa and a rented German car, the officials let them go to Germany on the condition that they would stay in the village right by the border. To them, this was preferable to staying in one of the camps in the cities. They also told us how the Czech secret police had checked their apartment just before they left.

There were worse stories told by refugees from some of the other socialist countries. A group from Romania, for example, had to swim across the Danube to escape. The boundary patrol shot at them. The three who made it knew that one of their group was shot to death. Another probably drowned, as they heard no news about him afterwards.

With increasing frequency, within our refugee group, people began to report strange dreams about their escapes. In the dreams, we would find ourselves somehow back in our homelands or would discover that our families were behind the Iron Curtain with ourselves desperately trying to join them there. In another type of nightmare, we would return for something stupid and be unable to get back to

Germany afterwards. Petr once dreamed that, instead of going to the restaurant for supper, he went back to Czechoslovakia to buy wieners and then realized that he could not return to us. These were our common nightmares, which as time passed, gradually tempered. We began to dream of finding our way back to our families and, after about a year, the dreams disappeared completely.

As winter approached, the local emigration office got more and more complaints, mostly due to the increasing cold. Ironically, the complaints came, not from refugees, but from the owners of hotels and bed-and-breakfast operations. They had thought that their arrangements with the government were to be short term, but now our stay looked like it would last nine months to a year. Most of the places were equipped only for the summer season, which finished in September. This was the case in our hotel, as we did not even have double windows. Those who had rooms to rent for winter, of course, preferred their winter guests rather than refugees.

The winter season started in December, so the local emigration office began to look for solutions in the fall, of course, without our knowledge. It came as a shock when they announced a decision to move us all to a big hotel at Königsee on December 1. Königsee is a well-known recreational area. One of Germany's two national parks is located near by. The park was about fifty kilometres from Aufham, in the southeast corner of Bayern, and already in the Alps. The village of Königsee is situated on the north shore of the lake, which bears the same name. The lake itself is eight kilometres long, one to two kilometres wide, so deep it was said to be bottomless, and deeply carved into the surrounding mountain sides. On the south side, it connects to another, smaller lake. Germany's second highest peak, Watzman (2713 m), towers close to the lake. Locally, the mountain is known as the "Watzman family" as the surrounding peaks look like a configuration of family members.

A lift connects the village to another peak, Jenner, where there were excellent ski runs in winter. In summer, the top of the lift marks a trail head for numerous mountain hikes. It was also famed for paragliding, a very popular sport at the time of our stay there. A new bob-sled track had been built in the village to accommodate the top national and international competitions. All these features made Königsee a major tourist destination. With the exception of farming, the whole village was oriented to tourist services. Countless shops, restaurants, attractions, and accommodations were offered, mostly catering to summer tourists. In winter, most of the small shops, restaurants, hotels, and bed-and-breakfasts were closed. Only a few large hotels operated. One of these had been specifically built as low-cost accommodation for young Germans, as otherwise everything was very expensive here. We suspected that even the young Germans were unimpressed with this four-story building, constructed of concrete blocks, and located behind a knoll in such a way that most of the rooms received no sunshine. In any case, the owner had offered it to the local emigation office, a ready-made solution to our housing problem.

Unfortunately for us, Königsee's focus on recreation made it unsuitable as a place for refugees to live. Everything was very expensive. The village did not have a school, so the children had to ride a bus to attend school in the next village. We adults, unable to afford the high prices in Königsee, had to walk to this village for shopping. Even food purchases were too expensive locally, so we regularly made a lot of trips out, on foot to avoid the cost of using the bus. If we had any business with the government offices, that meant a further five-kilometre walk.

Protests from all sides stemmed from the proposed move to Königsee. The refugees were worried about moving to a big hotel where 200-250 of us would be housed together, while so far we had lived comfortably in our small hotels, despite a little cold. Most of the objections, however, came from the residents of Königsee, who were concerned about the influx of so many refugees into their recreation area. Their protest grew until a local newspaper announced the possibility of a bomb in the hotel. After that, it was our turn to protest more loudly still, and to refuse to move. None of this had any effect on the government decision. No help for us came. Only the buses arrived, on schedule, to transport us to Königsee.

I remember the trip very well. Everybody sat with their possessions, packed in pack sacks, bags, or just bundles. It was a gray, cloudy day and Petr and I could not see much of the mountains, the only reason to look forward to this move. Occasionally, part of a peak appeared through the clouds and fog. However, the sight was not a friendly one, it appeared like an ominous barrier. When we finally arrived at the hotel, our spirits sank even lower. The cement floors had no carpets and the windows were without curtains. Our assigned room had a big patch of mildew on the floor and when we collected our blankets from the storage room, we found that they, as well as our mattresses, also smelled of mildew. The only bright spot was, when we compared this to our small hotel in Aufham, that nobody restricted baths or laundry. The big hotel had a big laundry and several shower rooms, to which we had free access.

More than half of the refugees were young, either singles or couples and their interests and routines differed from ours. They were up, partying, until late at night, then slept until late morning. There was poor sound insulation in the hotel, so there were many complaints and new orders from the hotel manager before approximately 200 people settled into a routine. If we had been unhappy with the food in Aufham, it was even worse at Königsee. The hotel did not have its own kitchen. Instead food was brought from a central kitchen, also under the same management, where food was prepared for a number of hotels. We often had the feeling that the leftovers were sent to our hotel, so we complained, protested, even went on strike, but nothing helped. The timing of the meals also created a problem for those of us with children. Breakfast was at eight, exactly the time when school started. As we had no kettles or stoves, their use being prohibited, we could not even warm milk for the children in the mornings. Lunch was served from 12:00 to 12:30. School was in session until 1:00 and then the children rode back to the hotel on the bus. Supper was always cold, a package handed to us together with lunch. The rooms had no refrigerators, so storage of milk and other fresh food presented a problem.

Petr and I never felt happy in this new situation. We had never been comfortable in a big crowd and now there was no escape from it. We did not like to kill time, engaged in fruitless talk with people who lacked goals or many interests. We restricted our socializing to those refugees known to us from the Aufham hotel and a few new acquaintances. With the children and our own preferences to consider, partying and visiting other refugees' rooms in the evenings did not appeal to us. There was nowhere else to go at Königsee after the children went to bed, as the hallways were unsuitable to sit in and the dining room was locked up after morning and noon meals. Petr and I reorganized our room, putting a wardrobe in front of the children's bunk beds. We bought a small lamp and kept quiet when Tom and Kate went to bed. I still believe that Kate weakened her eyes there, secretly reading in bed, in the half-dark.

We knew that it was important to come up with a routine that would help us to survive. We felt that it was a necessity for the children to have a sense of security. As we were unable to give them a sense of home, our family bonds had to become stronger than ever. As adults, we had more time on our hands than ever before. In Czechoslovakia, all adults were normally required to work by law, and even for women with small children it was nearly impossible to stay home. I was no exception and remember how sad I felt leaving my children each morning at a daycare, especially Tom, who was still a baby, and often cried when I left. Suddenly, it was the children who determined the time-table: when to get up, have breakfast, wait with lunch, help with homework. In the evening we would go for a walk, read, or play games. One change from the system in Aufham was that we did not need to walk the children to school as they rode there on the school bus and the driver was responsible for their safety.

We soon realized that the ability to cook some food on our own was essential. We bought an electric one-burner stove and very carefully hid it from the hotel manager, who, regularly as a watchdog, made patrols to check for use of prohibited stoves. Once I nearly burned through a night-table drawer when I tried to hide the stove, which was still hot. Several months later, after countless complaints, the government office responsible for us installed several stoves in one corner of the hallway. Now we could serve warm food to the children, as well as having the option of cooking our own supper if we preferred doing that to eating the day's cold supper. Later, Anita found us a small electric oven, so I would have even more menu options. Unfortunately, this also led to higher expenses for food. It was hard to look at the tempting vegetables and fruit for sale when I had so little money in my pocket and was all too aware how long it had taken to save even that much.

Petr had to do his carving in our hotel room, as we were unable to find other workspace as in Aufham. In the mornings, when the hotel was quiet, he worked using a handsaw, but in the evenings, when music from radios and record players mixed with the other hotel noise, Petr was able to use the drill. Nevertheless, we had to be very careful. The door was locked, insulated with a mattress, and an arrangement was in place so our friends could warn us if the manager was coming. Our German friends regularly supplied us with orders, so Petr was kept busy. I did not think of helping him with the rough preliminary work until after our move to Canada. However, I, too, was kept occupied with translation work and interpreting. I was also working to improve my English skills.

As a family, we continued our practice of hiking regularly. On most days, we did a "discovery" walk to explore our new environment. We planned longer hikes for the weekends. Unfortunately, higher elevations were already snow-covered, so we had to postpone the the real mountain trips until spring. We had no idea of how long we would be here or how much time there would be for such trips. In early December the village was quiet with parking lots empty and shops, restaurants and street markets closed. The boats, which took tourists on excursions, were in their winter shelters. St. Bartoloma's church, a major tourist attraction built on an inlet accessible only by boat, was closed until next summer. The nearest town, Berchtesgaden, was more lively, as more businesses were open there. However, the major tourist attractions near it, an old salt mine and Hitler's infamous mountain residence, the Eagle's Nest, were also closed. We had to wait until summer, to see how busy the area was when thousands of visitors were rushing to see the various attractions. So many places, which looked dull and abandoned in winter, were completely transformed in the summer. Years later, when I would listen to German folk music on CBC radio, I would be transported into the atmosphere of the lively music and activity surrounding the tables at outdoor cafés where tired visitors to Königsee could enjoy a refreshing beer and something to eat.

The children began to show some progress at school. In Aufham, there had been very few Czech children in the classes, so the teachers had not encouraged them to work harder. Now, with so many Czech and Slovak children in their new school, the teachers had to focus on them. Kate, with her natural ability, soon worked her way to the top of the class. I recalled how her picture had been taken for display on the "honor board" back in Czechoslovakia, just before our departure on holiday, and wondered how quickly it had come down when we did not return. Tom did not absorb his lessons as quickly as Kate and he quickly forgot things he had recently learned. I remember drilling Tom on the names of days and months in Czech and German during one of our afternoon walks. Surely, after two hours, he would know them. However, by the next day, he mixed up the order again. At least math was not a problem for him and he kept pace with his classmates. Both children liked to draw, a great advantage in the lower grades.

The effort to gain some friends definitely helped the children to overcome the language barrier. Within the first month, Kate made friends with a girl from a local farmstead. This connection helped all of us to feel more comfortable in the village. It took longer for Tom, but by spring he, too, befriended a boy from his class. At the hotel, Kate and Tom preferred to play with the friends that they had made in Aufham, especially the children from the other family that had decided to apply for Canada. Perhaps we helped a bit with their decision.

Behind the hotel, the children adopted a wooded area, with numerous rocks and boulders, as their playground,. The four of them made forts and built "houses" with tiny rooms. Unfortunately, from time to time, there were encounters with other children who came to destroy their work. My blood pressure went up, when I saw the apathy of the other children's parents to the situation. However, it was ultimately the children's problem and they had to defend the place themselves.

As Christmas approached we found ourselves being drawn into the local festivities. Back in Czechoslovakia, the government had tried to suppress the religious origins of Christmas. It was called a family feast and the emphasis was on shopping and generation of commercial profits. Here, in Bayern, the shops were still busy but there was a strong orientation to the Catholic church and an emphasis on the religious feast.

We had our first experience of the local customs relating to Saint Nicholas, the original European Santa Claus, on December 6, St. Nicholas Day. It was a Saturday, and our family had hiked to a nearby hill to enjoy the view of the foothills around Königsee. It was gray and cloudy and the sight of the lights coming on in the towns, villages, hamlets, and homesteads all around was a memorable one. In the Canadian mountains, buildings are rarely a part of the scenery as towns tend to be far apart and chalets and lodges are set in secluded hollows. In Germany, the population has increased many times through the centuries. As more and more people moved to distant places in the mountains, they began to use even the highest mountain meadows for farming. Single farmsteads slowly transformed to become hamlets, hamlets became villages, villages — towns. The number of individual buildings located along roads has steadily increased until one seldom drives through areas without habitation. Even nature has been adapted to human need. Forests have been harvested and carefully reforested through many centuries, as required by ancient forest law, so that succeeding generations continue to benefit from nature.

We were interrupted from our contemplation of civilization and nature by a strange noise coming from the closest farmstead. It looked like a swarm of sheaves and after a close look with the binoculars, we concluded that it must be part of a local St. Nicholas custom. This reminded us that the children had been promised St. Nicholas presents back at the hotel. On our return, it appeared that, indeed, St. Nicholas had come. It was the same character I remembered from my own childhood, a dignified figure with a long white beard in the red vestments of a priest. He had with him not only several angels, who had brought treats for the children, but also a crowd of devils. Their appearance reminded us of the sheaves we had glimpsed earlier as they were wrapped in straw, only with horns, long red tongues and rattling chains to show that they had come from hell. They produced a lot of noise and made the gathering a lively one, but the children clearly felt the uneasiness that combined with the pleasure of the occasion. Finally, each wonder-struck child was called up to receive a small package of sweets. It was a St. Nicholas day to remember!

We soon encountered more Christmas customs. The ceremonies that accompanied Advent on Sundays in Berchtesgaden were a popular tourist attraction. Musicians in local costume blew their long Alpine horns and other men, dressed in old forest uniforms, shot a salute using antique muskets. Then there was the church service, which ended with us all singing Christmas carols, a beautiful contribution to the festive atmosphere. The feeling of Christmas was reflected everywhere, especially in the decoration of the streets, shops and homes. We had never experienced it like this, as we walked around the town almost as wide-eyed as the children. Repeatedly, the wood-carving shops drew our attention, especially the beautiful and varied nativity displays which spoke so clearly of the purpose of all the bustle.

It was a joy to shop for Christmas gifts. There was none of the laborious hunting for presents that we knew from our homeland. The shop displays were very attractive and even though we had resolved to save our money we could not resist buying for ourselves and for relatives back in Czechoslovakia. By this time, we knew from family members who had stayed in touch with with us, how everyone had reacted after our escape. Because of the distance separating us when we still lived in Czechoslovakia, we were used to communicating by letter with Petr's mother and his sister, who lived beside her. Though his mother had shed tears when she found we had fled the country, it was at Christmas that she felt the loss most, as that had been the usual time for visiting. Petr's sister had even begun to send us gifts with her usual letters. She supplied us with hand-knitted sweaters, mittens, socks and toques, as she was very good with handicrafts. All these items were very welcome as they would have been expensive to buy locally.

Communication with my family was more sporadic. My sister did not write to me at all. My brother wrote occasionally in the first year, but then stopped, I suspect from fear and the influence of my brother-in-law, who was a member of the communist party. I missed them very much, especially my sister, who had been almost like a twin to me. We had been together in the same grade at school from the first grade to graduation, as she started school one year late due to illness. Later, our children had been born just a year apart and we had visited both her and my brother frequently. On this, our first Christmas out of the country, I sent gifts to the entire family through my brother.

It was my brother who related how our escape was discovered, giving us a good laugh through the description in his letter. He had tried to contact us, around the date of our expected return, because he wanted to visit. Unable to reach us, he decided to come in any case and en-countered the neighbors who had just discovered that our upstairs window, left slightly open to air the house, had been blown wide open by the wind. They climbed a ladder to close it, but when they looked in, found that the room was nearly empty. Worried that someone had broken in, they called the police, who upon inspection, judged that the dwelling was vacant rather than burglarized. When they confirmed that we should have been back from holiday by this time, they promptly sealed the house, right in front of the shocked neighbors and my brother. Within the year, our possessions were sold by the state.

7
Bavarian Christmas

"There is a cold or there is snow
And holly, fires and mistletoe ...
Church bells break the frozen air." — John Melling

The children had two weeks of leave from school for Christmas and most of the refugees who had friends or relatives in Germany were making plans to leave for the holidays. We were concerned that we would be spending Christmas in our crowded, noisy hotel until Anita and Tony thoughtfully invited us to their house. However, they also had plans to renovate during the holidays. Their house had originally been a cottage but they had enlarged it and made some improvements over the years. However, it was still too small and now they had decided to rebuild the house with a second floor to provide living space for other family members. This was a well-timed decision for their son, who married within the year and moved in with his new wife. Unfortunately, it also meant our stay could not be a long one.

Then, as we were worrying about where to go during the holidays, a forester we had met during the recent dog exams called us. After a talk with Anita, he invited us to stay with his family for a few days. He was willing to pick us up at our friends' place and to give us a ride back to Königsee afterwards, as they had a grandfather in a neighboring village and had planned to visit him in any case. We were surprised and very pleased to accept his invitation as it was not very common to invite strangers home, especially during Christmas. After all our dealings with the hotel and with government offices, we felt a bit second-rate as well as tired of hearing how thankful we should be for everything. Now it pleased us very much to be invited as friends, not as refugees, and to have the invitation also include Cir.

On the last Sunday of Advent, we arranged a visit in Aufham with Resi and Kurt's family and Cir. When we had lived there, we had been glad to accept their invitation to "stop any time" and had spent many happy hours together, especially on weekends. Often we took the dogs for walks, sometimes the children took advantage of the opportunity to watch television, which was not available at the hotel. It was hard for us, being unable to see Cir very often when we moved to Königsee. On this visit we brought presents, mostly Petr's carvings, which pleased our friends. We were surprised to find they also had beautiful gifts for us. Then it was time to take Cir back with us to Königsee, where we would keep him secretly in the hotel until Tony came for us.

Just before the holidays began, we experienced another surprise. Kate's school friend, Marianna, brought her a parting gift, a big box of home-made cookies. It had always been a tradition in our families to bake before Christmas. My grandmother went so far as to prepare twelve kinds of cookies. As we were not able to do any baking at the hotel, and the men in the family, especially, had a "sweet tooth," our joy over the box of sweets was enormous. We knew that Christmas baking in Marianna's family, one with five children, was a lot of work so we appreciated their thoughtfulness and willingness to share with us even more.

We arrived in Bad Tölz, with Tony, two days before Christmas. As Anita was working away from home, as well as dealing with the problems of the demolition at home, her time for food preparation was limited. I was happy to take over in her kitchen and thereby contribute to the seasonal feast. Of course, we found time for walks in the spa-town and for admiring its gorgeous decorations. Streets, markets, churches, shops, and private homes were all dressed up for the festivities.

It was the custom in Tony and Anita's family that people should not leave the table during the Christmas eve supper. If they did, it was sure to bring sorrow during the next year, so Anita tried very hard to arrange everything in such a way that we would stay at the table during the meal. Of course, right when we started, their friends came to wish us a happy season and afterwards their son came with his fiancee, then the telephone rang.... However, it was a very happy Christmas Eve as we exchanged gifts. All the time, we were aware of their friendship, and it was this that made the holiday so beautiful for us.

The next afternoon, Kaspar came to drive us to his forest district, located on the southern border with Austria. From the kitchen window, we could see the highest peak in Germany, Zuckspitze. The forest house, where the family lived, was one of only a few in the hamlet, with the rest also housing foresters and other forest workers. There was no farmland, as there was at Königsee, only the forest with the river below. We learned, to our surprise, that the river was not artificially regulated. Now, in winter, it trickled over a seventy-metre-wide gravel bed. During the spring melt, there would be deep rushing water from bank to bank. This was a most unusual sight, here in the middle of Europe. It was only later, in Canada, that we learned that rivers are mostly left to run in their natural course.

Kaspar's family lived on the second floor of one of the large traditional houses characteristic of this part of Germany, the first floor being occupied by forestry offices and a warehouse. The rooms upstairs were spacious, as was the kitchen, where a large wood stove dominated. The whole house was impressive and ancient, but also cozy due to the efforts of the inhabitants. I especially liked the woven rugs and baskets for dry flowers or just for mittens and toques, and the wooden plates, which were in daily use. With all the hunting trophies, paintings and pictures, the apartment reminded me of a picture from a hunting magazine, but everything was in the right place and though the furnishings appeared decorative, they were also useful.

We felt at home immediately and many things reminded us of life in our Czech hamlet. Kaspar's wife, Hilda, and I easily managed the daily household tasks and feeding the sheep and cleaning their pens. Petr and I also helped with daily chores in the forest, which included filling cribs and mangers with sweet-smelling hay, apples and dried food for the elk. On the edge of the forest, one morning, the herd waited impatiently for us to leave while we lingered, watching as the rising sun reflected off the fresh snow and lit the tops of the surrounding mountain peaks. This was delightful work and we were happy to take it over for the length of our stay here. Kaspar and Petr went hunting and our children were soon good friends with Kaspar and Hilda's children, running in and out as they played together.

The hamlet had a tiny chapel and mass was celebrated only occasionally. This was a last outpost before the Alps, with only six benches for seating inside the chapel, and additional visitors had to stand, either inside the door or out. Despite this, everyone looked forward to the Christmas Mass which, given the size of the chapel, was scaled down to the point where it felt like a family celebration.

On the first evening of our visit, the conversation turned to our escape and why we had taken such a risk. However, as evidence of their sympathy for us, our hosts soon invited us to stay until the new year, an invitation we were very glad to accept. We visited several other families with our new friends. One visit was to a family where the husband was on leave from his work overseas in Chile. He was a forester for an Austrian count who owned a huge tract of land, managed using forestry practices similar to those used in Europe. As this man wanted to move back home, he offered us his job when he learned of our situation. After quickly weighing the advantages and disadvantages, we refused his offer. We were looking for a new homeland for ourselves and the children, not just a place to work. We felt, in our hearts, that Canada would be our new home.

On January first, Kaspar's family gave us a ride back to Königsee. As they helped us with our luggage, they could not avoid seeing the remains of the New Year's Eve celebrations at the hotel — broken bottles and stained floor. Nothing was said, but they could feel the tension in the air. When we thanked them once more, they certainly understood our gratitude for the week we had spent with them.

8
Despairs and Hopes

"Hope is the thing that is left to us in a bad time." — Elwyn B. White

After New Year 1983, our application for immigration to Canada began its route through the bureaucratic process. We had sent off the required letter before Christmas and now began the impatient wait for an answer. In the meantime, we tried to collect more information and to make helpful contacts. Unfortunately, the initial responses did not look good for us. Our contacts gave us little hope for jobs or for immigration. The Canadian government, responding through the Czech office in Munich, regretfully confirmed this.

After our initial request to the Canadian government to support our application was denied, we appealed, but again were unsuccessful. We had not expected everything to go smoothly, nevertheless, we were very disappointed. The only other family we knew of, also applying for immigration to Canada, our friends from the hotel, were accepted. The Czech office explained that, this year, the Canadian government preferred those with professional engineering experience. Jan, a mechanical engineer, met this requirement, while we, as professional foresters, were not in demand. Unemployment among Canadian foresters and forestry workers was high now, especially in British Columbia, which has the greatest number of Canadian forestry positions. So, despite our assurances that we were willing to accept other employment, the door of Canadian government support for our immigration to Canada closed.

Our only other chance was to obtain a sponsor. The conditions for sponsorship at this time were that the sponsor could be a close relative (such as a parent or a child), a pool of five Canadian individuals, or one individual supported by a sponsoring organization. The sponsor had to guarantee their ability to provide financially for the newcomer(s) for at least one year, though the term could be extended to five years. The guarantee had to be in the form of a bank deposit, the required amounts being $2000 per adult and $500 per child — a total of $5000 for our family, to remain on deposit for the term of the sponsorship and to be used only in case of financial emergency. Our dream of going to Canada seemed unattainable when we learned of these conditions. We were more grateful than ever for our recent happy Christmas season as those memories sustained us through the stress and depression that we suffered during this difficult time.

We continued to follow up on all names and addresses that we had obtained from friends, or friends of friends, who had any connection to Canada. One of the people that we met this way was a man who had obtained Canadian landed immigrant status, but despite this preferred to live in Frankfurt. We found it startling that someone who had access to the space, nature and freedom, which we associated in our minds with Canada, would prefer to live within a small apartment, in a city skyscraper. The man, after we had gone to a lot of trouble to get to Frankfurt without the use of our own car, was not able to give us much information. However, he supplied the name, address, and telephone number of the Czech organization in Toronto, which was later a greater help to us. He recommended that we phone our contacts rather than writing to them, perhaps more convenient, but to us an expensive luxury when we were trying to save every penny possible.

In the fall, one of my first letters to Canada had been to a schoolmate from university who was living in Toronto. He had answered us right away, so now, turned down by the Canadian government, I wrote again to ask if he would be willing to sponsor us. We supplied the details of our financial situation, indicating that we would be able to use our savings for a major portion of the mandatory deposit, and assuring him that we were prepared to do anything that was necessary to support ourselves so that we would not be a financial burden to our sponsor. I had butterflies in my stomach as I mailed this letter, so crucial for determining the direction our lives would take.

During our time in Germany, it seemed that we were constantly in expectation of some news. Either we were waiting for news from home or letters that would determine the future course of events. The time that mail was expected to arrive at the hotel was the most important time of day and on most days a group of refugees could be found waiting in front of the hotel office. The hotel administrator in charge of our mail did not rush to distribute our letters, often excusing herself with a lack of time for mail sorting. Many times she did not "find" the letters until late afternoon, and so made her personal contribution to our continuing high levels of stress.

The refugees who planned to stay in Germany were also busy contacting friends and other leads in an attempt to find work. Those who had an offer of employment had a better chance of being able to leave the hotel to live on their own. The required document was the Azyl, the German landed immigrant status. Azyl granted the right to stay in Germany and to travel outside the country on a temporary passport, though travel to the Eastern Bloc was not recommended. Finding a job speeded the process of obtaining this official status and that requirement was what caused so much variation in the length of time refugees remained at the hotel. Invitations to appear for an interview in Zindorf were another type of letter for which everyone waited. At the interview, all documents — which had to include a certification that the applicant did not have a criminal record in Germany — were checked. In our case, the document came much later than was usual. Though government officials tried to assure us that having to wait several weeks for this clearance was not a cause for concern, Petr and I felt the stress of waiting for this additional documentation keenly.

Azyl was also required for those of us who did not want to stay in Germany, the difference in our landed immigrant status being that we would not be issued a work permit. Instead we would continue to be housed and fed at government expense. I do not wish to detract from all the help we received in this way, however, we wished to work and to pay for our own living expenses. Despite the new stoves in the hotel hallway, living conditions continued to be difficult. I generally used the illegal one-burner stove in our room rather than waiting to use one of the stoves in the hall and then being faced with cleaning it up before I could cook. The manager continued to search our rooms regularly, however, so using the stove or Petr's drill in our room was risky.

Parties and noise often continued beyond the official quiet hour, but our protests were ignored in favor of the good-looking young men who were also preferred if there was part-time work at the hotel. A lot of the residents did not take their cleaning duties seriously and the public areas began to look dirty as a result. As the first group of refugees gained their Azyl status, we hoped for some improvement. However, a new wave of immigrants arrived to take their place. From spring to summer 1983, the hotel was packed full to the brim. Though we met some interesting people and had some enjoyable discussions and visits at mealtimes or in people's rooms, as time passed we found that we felt desperate to leave the hotel.

When we had visited with Kaspar's family at Christmas we had noticed a large bunkhouse, owned by the forest district, not far from his home. Now, we wondered if this might not provide our opportunity to escape the hotel. According to Kaspar, the facility was used mostly in summer, by short-term help, and never to full capacity. Kaspar offered us two rooms there and said he would provide a personal guarantee to the government if we were allowed to move in. It was a tempting offer, as Petr would gain a quieter work environment and I would also gain some employment opportunities. We put in an application, filled with hope and new energy. We met with Kurt in Aufham, and he offered to intercede on our behalf by contacting the municipal government. Unfortunately, all this effort was in vain. We got our Azyl in the spring but were denied the right to work or to move from the hotel.

There was some hope soon after this, however. My friend Vasek replied from Toronto, offering to sponsor us under certain conditions. The main problem was money — we would have to deposit the $5000 guarantee in a Canadian bank. Vasek could offer Petr employment in his landscaping business and we could all live with his family, or the children and I could stay in their cottage about a hundred kilometres north of Toronto. A picture of the cottage, a nice bungalow with a stone chimney and located on a large rural property, was enclosed. To us, in our small, crowded hotel room, the image of this cottage was just a step from paradise, and we promptly put it on display as an incentive.

Vasek was planning to visit his parents in Czechoslovakia and would then be travelling through Europe, including Germany. We gladly accepted his offer to discuss the conditions of his sponsorship and agreed to meet him in Munich, which we felt would be most convenient for us. However, we had to make the usual complicated arrangements: first a permit to leave the hotel, then a ride with Tony from Königsee, finally a ride, found for us by Anita, with friends going to Munich and back.

Luckily, everything went smoothly and we met Vasek at the Munich railroad station. We had an hour and a half — so little time and our future at stake — before he was scheduled to leave on the next train. We had so many questions, and Vasek was the first person we knew who was living in Canada, our destination. What was more, I had not seen Vasek for eighteen years and he had lived in Canada for most of this time, so even with a common language, understanding each other was sometimes a problem. Fortunately, we were able to agree upon the principal issues. Vasek had already applied to sponsor us before his departure to Europe. We agreed to send the deposit money as soon as possible to Toronto. Petr agreed to work in Vasek's business, which employed five to ten workers, in the summer and to take the government-subsidized English language course during the winter. This meant that Petr would live in Toronto and the children and I would stay at the cottage, but this strategy would get us through our crucial first year in Canada. The only thing that was missing was agreement of a sponsoring organization to our arrangements. We hoped that the Czech association in Toronto would help, as they had already been contacted and Vasek promised to be in touch with them when he returned home. We hoped they would grant their approval, which we saw as a formality, at their annual meeting in May. Vasek was the one who was assuming the financial and personal risks in sponsoring us.

As it turned out, we had to wait a while for the results of that meeting. The date was postponed several times and no one rushed to let us know the outcome when it was held. Knowing how much depended on that single decision and how important it was to the fate of of our application, we were very impatient for an answer. After two months, we could bear it no longer and called a member of the association, with whom we had previously corresponded. We had been encouraged by his previous sympathetic response but now we were delighted to hear that the sponsorship had indeed been approved and papers submitted to the government office. He was surprised we had not yet heard from the secretary. Not long after our call to Toronto, we received official confirmation of our application from the Canadian Consul in Bonn. Finally, our case shifted from the sphere of dreams to the reality of administrative processing.

In the meantime, winter and spring had slipped by in Königsee. The lake did not freeze over, due to the unusually mild winter, so we did not realize our plans to travel on the frozen surface. Only Tom had a close encounter with the lake when he and a friend went to feed overwintering ducks and geese, including a flock of Canada geese, and Tom slipped on a landing stage and fell into the icy water of Königsee. Fortunately, some bystanders helped to get him out of the deep water and his friend led him home, half-frozen.

Right after New Year, I went with a bunch of flowers to say thankyou for the Christmas cookies. Kate's friend and her family lived on a farm about a kilometre from the hotel. Characteristically, for Königsee, the sloping meadows were bordered on the top by forest. The house, nearly 400 years old, and its barn were located in the middle of the pasture. The owners had added a small house, built in the same style as the old building, for their parents, on their retirement from active farming of the property. I learned later that while they could have hay from the meadow and even feed their cows in spring time, when summer came the cows had to be moved to higher pastures in the mountains. This was necessary because farmland had been subdivided many times over the generations so now there was not enough to assure sufficient hay for winter if cows also grazed there in the summer. Now in winter, with the cattle confined in the barn, the sloping meadow behind the house was the domain of the children. The Grassels had installed a simple lift with access directly from the house. All the children from their extended family met here for skiing and fun. To my surprise, Mrs. Grassel generously invited my children to join them.

Downhill skiing is an expensive recreational activity everywhere, and Königsee was no exception to the rule. It was easy to find used equipment, even the school provided it, but we could not afford to buy tickets. Only once, when a new chair-lift was opened on Jenner, the local mountain, did we get the opportunity to ski and ride the gondola free of charge. This was an opportunity that nearly everyone in the hotel took advantage of, at least to ride up for the view. Those who had found some equipment planned to ski down, and this group included our children, their good friends from the hotel and their father, Jan, who had promised to supervise the four children. When we got off the gondola at the top, and I saw how steep the hill was, I nearly lost my courage to let Tom and Kate ski down. They did not have any experience and these runs were not for beginners. However, they managed it and had a wonderful time, skiing the runs several times, losing track of each other, but meeting again at the gondola. Kate once skiied into the forest, fell into a drift, and had a hard time getting out. The group of us without skis climbed to the top of Jenner, above the gondola. We were surprised to find ourselves on top of a drift with the mountain wall going a hundred metres, straight down, below us.

At this point, Petr took a picture, which we still have, showing us dropped down into a crawling position, using our hands for support, as we reached the summit.

Petr and I skiied when we could on used cross-country equipment, though the division of land into small farms did not allow much room for trails. In contrast, our children often skiied by invitation at the Grassel's. Soon, they had arranged for their hotel friends to join them and the four of them were part of the winter fun which extended to include birthday celebrations, a masquerade ball, and even skiing on Jenner with the Grassel family. The children had a great time, and even I came to know the path to the farm well. I had arranged to buy milk and walked there every second day, usually with Ruza, whose children now shared milk, as well as fun, with mine. I practised my English, as Ruza knew the language well enough to help with pronunciation. When we stopped on a corner, milk jar in hand, it may have looked like we were gossiping, but it was Canadian provinces, territories and their capitals we were reciting, to learn Canadian geography and English pronunciation.

We did not see Cir or his host family very often due to our circumstances. From time to time, they visited or Kurt came to give us a ride to Aufham, always a welcome change from our routine. Once, in February, Kurt invited us and our friends from the hotel to come with him on a boat trip on the Königsee. He was relieving a workmate, whose duties included feeding the game near the lake. Before we crossed the lake to the feeding stations, we took advantage of having the boat to stop at St. Bartoloma's church. Afterwards, we helped Kurt with the feeding. No expensive tour would have given us such a pleasurable trip.

9
Try To Do the Best With Our Time

"Be contented with what you have got, and make the best of it; look on the bright side of things instead of the gloomy one." — Lord Baden-Powell

We were impatient with the slow progress of our application, but as we looked around at the mountains on our boat ride, we imagined ourselves hiking. We looked forward to spring and perhaps summer trips.

By March, the mild winter made way for spring. Snow at lower elevations and on the hills facing south melted first. As we walked, we could smell the thawing earth and awakening trees. In the shade, or at high elevations, we still floundered through snow. One warm April day, we set out for a lookout point above the middle of the lake. Our destination was actually above a vertical rock wall which rose straight up from the lake. The last portion of the trail was still under deep snow and it came above our knees as we sank into it. The view was beautiful — we could see St. Bartoloma church so far below that it looked like a child's toy. The light wind and spring sun were so warm that we were soon dry.

The children had another two-week holiday at Easter and Kaspar, again, invited us to Vorderriss. For the first week, we stayed in the bunkhouse, where we had hoped to reside instead of at the hotel. After that, we moved to a hunting cabin, located higher in the mountains. The cabin was a big one, with several rooms, but we chose to occupy only a small attic room because it was easier to heat and that left us with more time for trips. The game had moved to the grassy southern slopes and feeding them was unnecessary now so we hiked the wide creek bed and climbed the open hills for views, and did not mind at all when we ran into snow patches during our walks.

We had been reading the adventure book *Fast Arrows* with our children. It was a Czech book, written before the communist regime, and forbidden when they came to power. We had found a new reprint in Germany, and Kate and Tom just loved it. Inspired by the descriptions of how to collect badges for various achievements, Petr and the children decided to earn a badge for bravery, during our last week of holidays. Petr found a place in a small bowl to which they would have to come separately at night. There was a miniature waterfall which produced a fine mist that made the place look mysterious. The children even found the bones of a chamois (an Alpine goat) and the horns became a trophy attesting to their courage.

When we returned to Königsee, it made us unhappy again to exchange our beautiful solitude for the crowded hotel. This time, I resolved to do something about my forced inactivity. Of course, I had tried before to find a job and friends had tried to help, but it was still low season. Now, we found that the National Park Berchtesgaden had an exhibition at Königsee. Viewing their exhibition, I recalled my work with volunteers in the provincial park at home, and began to wonder if they would use volunteers here. I gathered my courage, and Petr and I paid a visit to the park headquarters in Berchtesgaden. They received us well, and when they found we had experience and wanted to work as volunteers in the field, we soon came to an agreement. They were just preparing a field project to study the effect of recreation on wildlife in the Alps and had just one student recruited to work on it so far. As two additional and experienced persons, willing to work for free, we were very welcome.

We found the work very rewarding. At last we could be outside, doing something we liked and adding to our knowledge of the park. After the first few days of observation, when park officers went with us, we were responsible for our own schedule and routines. The monitoring took place not far from the top of Jenner, in one of the small side valleys and away from the main trail. We usually sat on a large boulder which gave us a good view of the entire area. There was good cover and good grazing nearby, so we observed, mainly chamois, marking their movements every fifteen minutes and noting their activities, approaching hikers, response from the game, and so on. We also made a note of any other wildlife. The marmots amused us for hours and it was a pleasure to watch eagles and other birds of prey. The main monitoring objective was the chamois, however, and we learned a lot about them. It was an unforgettable experience to see a herd climbing a steep mountain wall together with their young.

Observations were done two or three times a week, though the personnel doing them could vary, with myself, Petr and the student taking turns going out in groups or individually. I enjoyed going out because I had the additional personal pleasure of observing alpine wildflowers from early spring to fall. This had always been my hobby and doing the volunteer work gave me a wonderful opportunity. I could not resist buying a wildflower guidebook in spite of the knowledge that it would be of little use to me in the future. It gave me pleasure to know the names of the flowers and I liked to test my knowledge on our family hikes on Sundays. Now, in spring, the meadows were full of crocuses and summer soon brought gentians into bloom (including a valuable purple variety which was covered with small black dots, the roots of which were used to produce a liqueur). It was unforgettable to see vast areas covered with the red alpine rhododendron, called Alpenrose. In fall, the slopes and meadows took on a rich purple color from the many varieties of asters. It was simply beautiful.

We gained an additional benefit from our work. As the monitoring was done on the top of Jenner, we were given tickets for the gondola, but after a while, because we were so well-known to the operators, they often forgot to ask for tickets. Sometimes, we walked down at the end of our day, and so our tickets accumulated. We used them to take trips with Tom and Kate and also gave them away to friends. Once we gave four tickets to a young family whose mothers had come from Czechoslovakia to visit them. (That was the only way for parents to see their escaped children. Officials would issue permits for the visit if the parents declared that they could convince the escapees to return home.) We enjoyed the description of their trip. All four of them had ridden up on the gondola, using the tickets, and enjoyed the view immensely. However, not having return tickets, they had to walk down and both the mothers, being city people and not in the best physical condition, found this to be the most challenging experience of their trip to Germany. They even forgot to lament over their children's escape or to apply pressure to return home.

Taking the gondola to the top of Jenner made higher-elevation hiking more accessible and we took advantage of the opportunity as soon as we could. We enjoyed the mountains from many different points of view, discovered new valleys where only summer barns indicated other visitors, paddled close to waterfalls or climbed steep rock walls. Always, on these occasions, we wondered — how would the Canadian mountains look to us?

When we visited with Kurt's family after Easter we spoke with enthusiasm of our stay at the hunting cabin. They were surprised we had enjoyed it so much, but to our delight, asked if we would like to spend some weekends in the cabins near Aufham. We welcomed any weekends away from the hotel, and eventually visited most of the cabins in Kurt's hunting area and some of those near Aufham, where he also had access. We were surprised to discovered that a particular area near Aufham was prime grouse habitat. With our recent memories of these birds in Czechoslovakia and our unhappiness at their decline, we were excited to observe ten males in one spot. They performed their courtship ritual in the forest clearings, even when the sun already shone through the trees and highway traffic could be heard in the distance. It all felt very strange to us. Kurt later told us that grouse populations had also declined here, with the result that hunting the birds was forbidden about ten years before. Now their population had begun to climb. Unfortunately, the decline in Czechoslovakia was not due to overhunting but to changes in habitat, while in this part of Germany, the grouse survived despite the increased pollution from the highway and no one paid much attention to them.

Later in the spring, Kurt started to build a garage and Petr offered to help. As a result, he stayed for a while in Aufham and enjoyed the beautiful spring days at work on the garage and out in the field with Kurt. Another time, Petr did some woodcarving decoration at Kurt and Resi's house, providing another chance for a change of scene. I also found work, helping in a small hotel kitchen in Königsee, doing their laundry and other odd jobs as needed. Suddenly, our days were very busy and it was fortunate that Jan and Ruza could help us with the children. Then, someone from the Grassel family gave Kate a bike, which soon became a source of pleasure for all four children.

In this region of Germany each religious holiday was accompanied by an extended school holiday. So, in June, the children got fourteen days off for Pentecost. This time, we spent just a few days at one of Kurt's cabins. We had our volunteer positions on the National Park project and Petr continued his carving and I had my job at the hotel.

With so much time off for holidays, school was not scheduled to finish until the end of July, a very impractical arrangement due to the summer heat. Often school would be called off after only a few hours if temperatures rose above thirty degrees Celsius, the limit for keeping school in session. The outdoor swimming pool at Schönau, where the school was located, became the most popular place on these days. When the pool had first opened in June, we were in doubt whether to buy a swim pass for the summer, as we were not certain how much we would use it. In the end, we were glad we had bought a family pass, as we used the pool extensively until it closed in September. It was a gorgeous feeling to paddle in the warm water, soak in the sunshine and to watch the surrounding mountains, with the tops still white with snow.

At the start of summer, many of the hotel inhabitants were packing to leave Königsee. The first to leave were a young couple going to Australia in March. After that, a small group went to the United States. By June, many of the original group were gone, including our friends who had obtained Canadian government sponsorship. They had decided to go to Ontario, where they had friends. As we said good bye and wished them the best, we could not help worrying about our own application and whether it was moving through the proper channels. New people soon filled the empty rooms, leaving us, as the longest inhabitants, feeling somewhat lost.

From one family of newcomers, we learned of a tragic crossing at the Yugoslav-Austrian boundary, exactly where we had crossed a year ago. This family of four, with two boys aged eleven and thirteen, had met a young couple with a baby just as they began to walk toward the border. Having the same goal, they joined forces, with the first family helping the young couple with their luggage. Suddenly, they heard a whistle, followed by gunshots, and everybody ran, the two boys straight ahead, without stopping. The mother, still trembled as she told how she watched the soldiers for a long time from her hiding place among some young trees, until she found the courage to continue ahead. She still carried a bag belonging to the couple when, relieved, she encountered first her husband and then their sons. Even when they lingered, for a dangerously long time, hoping the young couple would come, they remained missing. Finally, the family of four abandoned the luggage and continued their trek toward Austria. Later, when they tried to get news, they learned only that two people had been shot to death near the border. None of the stories lifted our mood and confirmed only that the road back was definitely closed.

Finally, in the middle of the summer holidays, the long-awaited summons came from the Canadian Consulate in Bonn. Although it was clear our departure would not be prompt, the letter filled us with happiness. After months of uncertainty, we at last had some confirmation in our hands. We immediately began to plan our trip to Bonn.

Kate and Tom could stay with Anita and Tony, as their house was partly finished by now. We could go by train as far as Karlsrühe, where Petr had a cousin. She and her family had been living there since their escape seven years ago. Now, after exchanging letters, we looked forward to our reunion.

We were warmly welcomed in Karlsrühe, and the next day continued by train to Bonn. Petr couldn't find words to praise the German trains enough for cleanliness, comfort and, above all, punctuality. The railroad to Bonn ran through the beautiful Rhine River valley. The river cut deeply into the hillsides in some places. On the hill tops were old fortresses, at lower elevations, castles. If the slopes were accessible, they were covered by vineyards. On the river, we saw boats of all sizes from small recreational craft to large cargo ships. Perhaps it was because of our happy mood, through which we perceived the landscape, but we still remember the trip as a lovely one.

In Bonn, we found that the Canadian Consulate had mistakenly placed us with a group from Poland, with the result that there was no Czech translator. I did not have the courage to try my English, in spite of my daily efforts to learn it, but we managed the interview comfortably in German. The officer in charge of the proceedings was pleasant and we admired him as a "real Canadian." The application from our sponsors in Canada was approved. We now needed to arrange for medical exams and visas to Canada, along with the required documentation. Afterwards, the Canadian Consulate, in cooperation with the German government, would reserve our air tickets to Canada. This statement was like "music from paradise" to our ears. In the end, he wished us a successful life in Canada and personal luck for our whole family. In answer to our question, "When can we expect our departure?" we at last had a clear time frame after all the previous uncertainty. Though the reply was, "Not before the end of September," we felt filled with a new zest for life and what our future travels might hold.

In a cheerful mood, we organized our schedule for the rest of the summer at Königsee. It turned out to be a very hot summer, with the temperature climbing to forty degrees Celsius, the hottest recorded in 200 years. By mid-summer the water in the lake near the hotel was warm enough to swim in, though we found we were quite busy and short of time. Petr wanted to finish all the orders he had received for carving, we had our volunteer work on the park project, and I had the challenge of getting out of the hotel unnoticed to go to my job. As more refugees arrived, we were not sure who could be trusted, and I was increasingly worried that someone would disclose that I had a job. Once, while I was doing my laundry, I got quite a scare from one of the newcomers who began to shake me when I hesitated over my reply to her questions about finding employment.

At the end of the summer we transferred most of our savings to Canada. We would bring the rest with us on the plane. Right before departure, we decided to go shopping for something special for each of us. I bought myself a typical German dress dirndl which I had admired in the shop window all summer long. We made a long-planned circuit of the lake (about forty kilometres) and climbed Watzman. All our trips included Kate and Tom, who were excellent hikers. The last asters were blooming on the hills around Königsee when we finished the National Parks job in September. They thanked us for our work and wished us good fortune in Canada. Unfortunately, their best wish, that we find similar work in Canadian national parks took a long time to be realized.

As time passed, the number of friends from home willing to keep in touch with us declined, though from time to time we still got some news. Some of it was sad, like that concerning the speed with which the dry-up of the Czech forests continued and how beetle infestations added to the destruction. Other news concerned our private lives, such as the sale of our possessions in the town near our original home. Petr's mother was informed that a court in Ostrava would handle our crime of escape and pass judgment, though no final verdict was ever announced. We did learn that the length of a sentence depended on level of education: people with college education would typically receive one to two years, while those with a university degree would be sentenced to three years in prison in the event that they returned to Czechoslovakia. Other circumstances were also considered, resulting in a sentence of six years for our friend Jan. However, these things did not mean much to us as we were increasing absorbed by thoughts of our future and the long-awaited trip over the Atlantic.

September arrived and we received notice that our departure to Canada would be on September 27. Again there were obstacles to overcome. There was a problem about our dog. The clerk in Munich had originally noted that we wanted to take Cir with us, but as we did not repeat this information, nobody marked it when tickets were issued. We had to telephone, negotiate, and eventually pay for a ticket to transport him. We were more fortunate than some of the other emigrants, though, as we did not have to repay the funds advanced for the rest of our tickets. Afterwards, we laughed about how Cir had the most expensive ticket.

Our final difficulty related to sending some of our possessions to Canada ahead of time, something that we badly wanted to do as we were depending on public transportation to get to the airport. We had been advised that the exchange rate (one Canadian dollar to two Deutschmarks) would make Canada expensive for us, making it desirable to have as many basic necessities as possible beforehand. Finally, everything was arranged and it was time for farewells.

Kurt and Resi, with tears in their eyes, gave us gifts and 50 DM to call them as soon as we landed with news of how the trip had gone for Cir and ourselves. It was very sad to part from the dog as they had grown very close over the last year. We all worried about whether we would have problems with quarantine, and Kurt and Resi even offered to fly Cir back to Germany rather than have him endure quarantine, as we knew that some dogs died under conditions of such severe over-crowding and stress. A veterinarian assured us that regulations had recently changed and that Cir would have no problem with access to Canada if all his shots were up to date. We still worried, but fortunately the vet was right.

Kaspar's family invited us to their house for a final visit. As we had not seen them over the summer, this was our first opportunity to see Cir's offspring, as the mother was Kaspar's bitch. Our children and the puppies running wild through the hamlet injected fun and joy into the occasion.

Even many of the hunters and foresters for whom Petr had carved gun shafts and antler jewelry came to say goodbye. We stopped at Tony and Anita's new house on our way to Munich and found them hard at work finishing the interior. Anita gave me a pearl necklace and worried that this could be the last time we would see each other. I tried hard to reassure her, and also myself, that we would definitely meet again. Several years later, a friend from Calgary made a business trip to Germany. I felt almost envious of him and also wanted to go, to visit our German friends. Curiously, I was not homesick for Czecho-slovakia.

It was Octoberfest in Munich when Kaspar drove us to the railroad station. The streets were busy with festively dressed people, visiting attractions, carousels, pubs and beer gardens. However, all of Kaspar's family looked sad and, again, the tears showed up. We were very thankful for everything they did for us, but mostly for their friendship.

The train took us to Karlsrühe, where we met the family of Petr's cousin and also his uncle. He had just come from Czechoslovakia for a visit. It was a very pleasant time, but our thoughts were already on the way to Canada. On the next day, we took a train to Frankfurt. I only reget that we do not have a family picture of our departure. We had to make our way from the Frankfurt railroad station to the airport by public transportation (including riding on escalators) with all our belongings. Our biggest piece of luggage was a metal box bought on Vasek's recommendation. Two of us had to carry it and it must have made a funny picture. There I was, in high heels, one hand on the handle of the box, our dog's leash in the other, nervously looking out for the children. Kate and Tom certainly looked forward to the trip. It would be an adventure and an interruption of school. Through the whole past year, they had shared in the waiting, disappointments and renewed hopes. Even if they did not grasp everything, we had discussed our plans and progress openly, because they were also participants in our adventure. On the way to the airport, they both carried their school packs, filled with their possessions, and joyfully marched forward to continue our "big trip." Because they had never flown on a plane before, it was even more of an adventure for Kate and Tom. Though Petr had not flown either, he did not not show such enthusiasm!

At the airport we made all the necessary arrangements, which included purchasing a cage for Cir, before our flight. We closed him into it with some anxiety. Petr left his hunting jacket in the cage so Cir would know we were close. Then he was taken to the luggage area. While we waited, I got the idea to call my sister. Even though she did not share my happiness, that we finally were on our way to Canada, it did not matter — my mood soared high. On September 27, 1983 at 13:40 we left Europe and after more than a year of waiting, we were on our way to Canada, the country to which we wanted to go.

10
Canada!

"The true North strong and free..."
— from the Canadian national anthem

The trip was a long one and I remember how hot it was in the plane, as I was wearing a wool dress and felt uncomfortable. Our seats were in the middle section, so most of the time we saw only clouds when we looked toward the windows. Just above Iceland, we caught a glimpse of the strange treeless land below us. Then just before Toronto, the clouds disappeared and we viewed, with astonishment, the regular squares and rectangles of land which surrounded the city. We had noticed these on maps as well, the result of roads mostly laid out at right angles to each other, on a grid, and not crooked, like European roads. Only lakes interrupted the human symmetry here.

We landed at 16:00, Toronto time, after a flight that had lasted nearly ten hours. We felt betrayed when our fantasy of how we would first touch Canadian soil was replaced by the unromantic reality of a moveable tunnel attached to our plane to lead us directly, without allowing up to step on the ground, to a check-in hall.

As we had arrived in a German plane, most of the travellers were German. I remember a group of young people who pushed their way through other travellers to the wicket where they noisily showed their passports. To their surprise, the clerk froze them with strict words, "No German, English please!" We found some humour in their new serious manner and difficulty as they painfully tried to express themselves in English. Our memories of how we had been handled in Germany, "If you don't speak German, it's your problem!" were still fresh; now, suddenly, German was not the most important language.

I have to admit, however, that I was not much better with my English than the young Germans. Even after a year of practice, I did not have much confidence, so I laboriously composed each sentence before I spoke it aloud and I struggled to understand words spoken to me. I was also very nervous, with recent memories of previous border crossings, full of strain and suspicion. Now we had to go through Canadian Immigration with no idea of what procedures to expect, so I hoped we would meet Vasek first and have his help. Unfortunately, this was not to be. When I explained, with difficulty, our reason for entry into Canada, the clerk at the wicket immediately directed us to the Immigration office.

Our discussion there was definitely not an easy one. The clerk was not one of those people who offer help or ask leading questions. She simply examined our documents and waited for my laborious explanations. She seemed to lose patience at times and I was sure that she was noting that only applicants with good English should be accepted in Canada. Of course, none of this helped me, as I struggled for the right words and the strength to explain that we had just come from another country where we had been forced to communicate in a different, unfamiliar language. However, the outcome is the most important aspect of any discussion, and we were given Landed Immigration papers in the end. From this time it would be a wait of three years until we could apply for Canadian citizenship. To our amusement, our Immigration papers were stapled to our old Czech passports, which were valid only in Yugoslavia. A paragraph in these passports states "The citizen is under protection of the Czech Socialist Republic." For the next three years these would be our most important papers. With them, we would not have the courage, even if we had the money, to cross the Canadian border. Only Tom and Kate would have acceptable papers, as they had received new passports in Germany.

After we left the Immigration office, we had to have our luggage checked, and then another important officer awaited us, the veterinarian. He questioned us on the names of compulsory shots. We showed Cir's vaccination certificate, but unfortunately the terminology was not the same in Germany as in Canada. The vet just wanted to mark off the shots on a chart, so he asked us again for the names but I did not understand, forcing him to repeat himself. After three tries, I started to sweat and he started to swear. Meanwhile, Cir, whose cage was positioned behind the counter so that we could not see into it, recognized our voices and the wagging of his tail sounded like drumbeats against the cage. What a relief it was to know that he was fine! Finally, we satisfied the veterinarian's questions and were permitted to open the cage, joyfully ending our dog's solitary confinement.

We collected our belongings, even the impractical cage, and proceeded out of the restricted area. Behind the rope of the check-in hall, Vasek and his wife, Beatrice, waited for us. It was a comfort, after the lengthy travel and unpleasant administrative experience, to know that someone was waiting for us. We were delighted to hear their first words, "Welcome to Canada!"

In our imagination Canada was, above all a place of vast natural space, of huge forests and lakes, a small human population, with, somewhere in the background, mountains, where we hoped to end our long journey. Toronto, as a city, did not correspond to such a vision. As I have mentioned, we did not much like cities and we never felt free there. Now we were to have our first experience of Canada in the centre of a city. Vasek lived in an apartment block, to us, a "sky scraper." His was one of several buildings which formed a large complex interconnected by pedestrian pathways which ran through park-like lawns and plantings. Parking and laundry facilities were underground and one of the buildings housed a recreation centre and swimming pool, as well as several banks, services, and convenience stores.

Vasek and his employees maintained the green space here and at several other parks and private gardens. As most of his work was in and near this complex, he and his wife found living here very convenient.Their apartment had two bedrooms, a large living room and kitchen. They had recently rented one of the bedrooms to a teacher from China, so they were sure another tenant, in this case, Petr, would not mean any inconvenience to them. Vasek and Beatrice actually gave the whole family the opportunity to stay with them in Toronto. This would have offered the advantage of having school, shopping and offices all close by instead of the isolation we could expect living at their cottage without the use of a car. However, I immediately rejected the idea. There is a difference between having a single tenant and having a family of four with a dog. Vasek and Beatrice had once had a dog, but they were not used to children, so I judged we would be wise to avoid potential problems. Our arrangements would only be for a year — surely we could manage at the cottage as previously agreed.

After the festive supper to welcome us, we made plans for the next few days. We had paperwork to complete relating to our immigration and needed to apply for an English course for Petr, but afterwards we could go to Lake Scugog and the cottage. There we would register Kate and Tom at school and make transportation arrangements for them.

As we looked out at the city from our friends' 36th-floor apartment, the view was like that from a lookout, especially as Toronto lays on a flat. Vasek proudly stressed how much green area we could see in the city, but we noticed most how the city lit up, as it was now growing dark. But Vasek got our full attention when he pointed out Lake Ontario — we were very close to one Canada's Great Lakes!

Over the next couple of days we were immensely grateful to Vasek, who not only accompanied us to the various government offices, knowing all their locations, but also did most of the talking. My discussions at the airport with the Immigration clerk and the veterinarian had damaged my self-confidence and I felt only despair about how long it might take me to learn the English language. However, the clerks and officials we saw were kind and displayed no reservations about our poor English. Our deepest impression in those first days in Canada was of the mix of human races: Chinese, Black, Caucasian, East Indian, Palestinian — all citizens of this large country, Canada.

Toronto did not look like any city we knew in Europe, as it spread out over a large area, with most citizens living in their own houses. Of course there were apartments, but these tended to be individual buildings or complexes surrounded by green space, not located in row upon row along the street as in European cities. There was no historic core, instead skyscrapers and office towers occupied the city centre, as they do in most North American cities. Another novelty for us was the use of plywood for construction, not brick or cement panels or blocks as in Europe. Some of the older houses already showed signs of wearing out, with sinking roofs and sagging porches; yet each had a tiny, carefully maintained area of lawn. There were a lot of trees in parks and near houses in wealthier areas. From our lookout in the apartment, with the benefit of daylight, we saw how whole areas were hidden in greenery, and liked the city for this attribute.

The offices which we had to visit were located in the business district and we were surprised not to see any shops or window displays. I remember seeing only one shop on our route. It sold used furniture and had a display of broken chairs at the entrance. This seemed like a marked contrast to the German towns and cities we had been in recently and their emphasis on window displays to lure passers-by into the shops. A few days later, Beatrice took me to a nearby shopping mall, and I discovered that the range of goods I had been expecting to see in the city centre was offered, but in a different way.

I found that shops here tended to be much larger, so knowledge of the location of items became important. I also found that I was not familiar with quite a number of products, among them peanut butter, instant breakfast foods, soup in cans, and various types of fish and cheese. I would have to learn not only the English names of familiar goods and new products, but also their packaging and organization within the stores. With restricted time and dependence on Vasek for transportation, shopping became a new source of stress rather than a pleasure. I was very grateful, in the weeks to come, to Beatrice for her help and advice.

While in Toronto, we visited the representative of the Czech organization who had signed as our co-sponsor. Above all, we wanted to thank this thoughtful man in person, as we believed he had greatly influenced the group's decision to help us. Both he and his wife were very nice to us. But I was somewhat shocked at her reaction to the flowers I had brought for her, "You should not do it! You don't know yet, how hard a time you will have, but you will see!" They had fled Czechoslovakia after the communist takeover in 1948, so their views of the country and people were different from our more recent experience. On the other hand, despite our gratitude to the organization for sponsorship, we could not conceive of joining it ourselves.

11
The Cottage

"No one ever studies language enough, for it is the home of all meanings." — Jean-Paul Desbiens

At last, we had attended to the required official matters and could leave for the cottage. The goal of the cottage, symbolized by its photograph, had sustained us in Königsee. Now, along with the children and Cir, I looked forward to seeing it at last. We knew that the location was in farming country, but we hoped we would also get our first glimpse of Canadian nature as we drove there.

At the end of September, it was still warm in Toronto, but the morning fog came in off the lake. On this morning, as we left the city behind, there was fog everywhere. No matter how hard we tried to see through it, we hardly recognized the change when we left the last of the suburbs. However, after a while the fog began to lift and we could see meadows, fields, groves, and houses with their mailboxes by the road. Everything was new to us and we wanted to see and know as much as possible. We were especially captivated by the sight of a strange tree, the American Elm. We soon learned its shape as a characteristic landmark in the farm country north of Toronto.

The cottage was located about 100 kilometres north of the city, on the northwest end of Lake Scugog, which was about twenty kilometres long. The end of the lake was reedy and surrounded by forest. Here was a wild island of nature in the farmland, its observation about to become a source of much pleasure. We would live just a few steps from the lake and behind our cottage was just one other building, the year-round house of a friendly older couple. Beyond this was a meadow, fenced by split eastern cedar arranged in a criss-cross fashion.

The cottage looked exactly as we had expected. It was located on the upper part of the oblong lot, which sloped gently down to the lake. The yard served Vasek for his landscaping business, as he grew seedlings of trees here, which he later transported to Toronto. The cottage itself had two bedrooms, a kitchen, bathroom and large living room with a door leading to a porch. After a full year spent living in a single room, the space of the cottage seemed palatial to me. Best of all, a huge fireplace dominated the living room. I had always imagined a fireplace as the centre of a household, but unfortunately, I had never had one until now. There was also a basement, which served as a garage and cellar. Vasek was still in the process of enlarging it, something made possible by the soft sandstone on which the cottage stood. In fact, Vasek had built the whole cottage himself and was rightly proud of his work.

During those first days, in spite of our longing to immerse ourselves in our first experience of Canadian nature, we were so busy that we hardly had time to take a dip in the lake. There was a lot to be done to arrange things so that the children and I could live without transportation when Petr and our friends returned to Toronto. The cottage was located in a recreation area, where only a small percentage of houses were used for year-round living. The closest village, only a tiny centre for the surrounding farms, with a general store, a church and a winter hockey rink, was seven kilometres from Vasek's cottage. The town of Lindsay was twenty kilometres away.

First, we had to do the week's shopping and try not to forget anything. Afterwards, with the help of our friends, we registered Kate and Tom at the local school. It was about fifteen kilometres from the cottage, a typical rural school, serving children from the farms and recreation areas around the lake. This was our first experience with a system of school bus transportation. Our children would board the bus at a stop about seven minutes from the cottage, the first stop on the route. It would take about three quarters of an hour for the bus to travel the remainder of the route, some thirty to forty kilometres, collecting the other children, before reaching the school.

Vasek arranged for a telephone line to the cottage so that we could be connected with the outside world. Despite the practicality, the ringing of the telephone was also a source of stress. Who would be calling? Would the caller speak Czech or English? If it was English, I usually had difficulty with the caller's name and their reason for calling.

We also had a very pleasant visit in Lindsay during those first few days at the lake. Besides Vasek and another university classmate, I also knew a teacher from my university who had resided in Canada since 1968. He lived in Lindsay and taught at the forestry college there. He was one of the first people to whom I had written when we arrived in Germany and he had given me Vasek's address, though he had expressed pessimism in regard to our chances of finding a job. His experience showed that it was difficult for forestry students to find work and so he had advised us to stay in Germany. Now that we had arrived in Canada, however, they made us very welcome. For the children and myself, at the cottage, they were now close neighbours and often helped us whenever needed. Helen, the teacher's wife, realized how disoriented I could be, as a newcomer, and helped me find my bearings. She not only assisted me with opening a bank account, she helped me with shopping and sometimes took us out to a restaurant or a McDonald's (another new experience).

Most important of all, she found a way for me to study English. First, she registered me in a correspondence course. This was not the best way for me to learn, unfortunately, as I needed to speak, to listen, and to learn pronunciation. Helen continued to look around and finally decided the best way would be to register for the special English class at the Lindsay High School. Transportation would be by school bus, a convenience, but also a problem as I was now committed to spending the entire day at school. To comply with school district procedures, I had to fill the rest of the day with other subjects, so I chose Biology 9, Social Studies 10 and another English class. Unfortunately, I could not advance to other classes, only to Grade 11, where the curriculum focussed on Shakespeare. His 17th-century English proved to be beyond my capabilities. Fortunately, I knew the Shakespearean plays, in translation, from reading or seeing summer festival performances in Prague's Royal Gardens, so I was not totally lost. I appreciated the opportunity of learning Canadian history in the Social Studies class and was quite comfortable with Biology.

My classes were held every second day, so on these mornings, I rushed to the bus stop with Kate and Tom. I find it hard to express how it felt to be back at school after twenty-five years, sitting at a desk with thirteen- to sixteen-year-old students. I had to cooperate with them, respond to the teachers' questions, do quizzes and write tests. Often, though I knew the answers, I was not able to express myself quickly in English. Luckily for me, all the tests were written ones, not oral as in Czechoslovakia. With the help of a dictionary, I was able to write my answers.

The special English class was completely different; here I was expected to speak directly with the teacher. Usually there were a few other students who needed help to catch up on their studies in various subjects, but generally, the teacher devoted a great deal of time to me.

We read easy books so I could listen and correct my pronunciation. The teacher reviewed the words which he considered more difficult and I tried to grasp their meaning, at first with a lot of help from my Czech-English dictionary, in which I looked up almost everything. However, with time, I began to understand more and more and could talk about each chapter in my own words. Language tapes were also a great help, as not only did I hear the correct pronunciation, I benefitted from listening for meaning in spoken English. So my study of English at high school was successful, as well as inexpensive, though I would not want to repeat the experience.

Just before Vasek, Beatrice, and Petr returned to Toronto we had an unusual excounter with our neighbors, Mr. and Mrs. Mason, an older couple originally from Britain. Vasek and Beatrice had told us how they sometimes called on them for advice, visited together, and were good friends. However, on this occasion the husband had spotted the children playing on the edge of the lake, in and around Vasek's wide-bottomed rowboat, and though they were in no danger, they were not wearing regulation life jackets. The neighbor was ready to call the police and Vasek had quite a hard time talking him out of it. From Mr. Mason's point of view, we had been neglecting the children's welfare. The episode frightened me — we might be breaking other laws in our ignorance of them, not to mention what kind of relationship would we now have with these neighbors? Happily, my fears were unfounded, as our ability to communicate improved, they were most helpful and supportive. The wife was, in fact, the first person on whom I tried out my fledgling English. I recall my frequent frustration when despite my repetition of some word, she still did not understand me but when I showed her the word in the dictionary, it turned out to be only a question of pronunciation.

Our lives soon settled into a pattern. Petr worked during the week in Toronto for Vasek and on weekends he came to the cottage with Vasek and Beatrice. The wage for landscaping work was not high, as the positions were usually filled during the summer by students, but it was enough to live on. When Petr started his language classes in November, we had just enough money coming in to buy food and other necessities, pay our telephone bills and sometimes contribute gas money. We were thankful that we did not have to pay rent as we could not afford it.

Looking back on these experiences, we see that we probably should have started differently. Maybe we should have overcome our dislike of the city, found inexpensive accommodation, and both worked. At the time, though, it seemed impossible to strike out on our own without knowledge of the language or any experience in our new country. We knew so few people, and whenever work opportunities were discussed, it looked black. The difficulty was demonstrated for us when, his language courses finished, Petr tried to find other employment. I also see that the planning that we had done in Germany, and the allowance that Petr received while attending courses, limited our desire to search for other options. So Petr endured his solitary life in the city.

On the other hand, the children and I enjoyed the freedom and solitude of country life. We had the opportunity to track and observe wildlife, including beaver and turtles which lived in the lake, and which we had never seen before. The entire area was a paradise for birdwatching, and I saw many new, as well as familiar, species. There were plentiful grouse, hares, and coyotes at our end of the lake. So I learned new species of animals and plants along with my new vocabulary.

Farms in this area were often separated by strips of deciduous forest, predominantly maple. Later, in the spring, we found it interesting to observe how farmers in the area tapped maple trees for syrup. Swampy areas were covered with eastern cedar, which apparently survives even in shallow water. The forest at the end of the lake had the greatest diversity of trees, including Douglas fir, eastern hemlock, spruce and many deciduous varieties. On my walks with Cir, I also found a number of abandoned farmsteads. Many of these had fruit trees around the location of the original house and though the trees had been neglected for years, they still bore fruit. I was able to collect a lot of apples and used them to cook everything I could imagine: bread pudding, apple dumplings, cakes and pies, preserves and juice. I dried a quantity of them for snacking and stored the best fresh ones in the cellar for winter eating. On the weekends, we all picked more apples so that Vasek and Beatrice could take some back to Toronto. Petr has a huge appetite for apples so the abundant apples were welcome. Our neighbor showed me how to make excellent jam and juice from the wild grapes which also grew in the area. The jam became a great favorite and I made a habit of looking for grapes on outings with Cir.

Once, as I was reaching for some grapes, I caught sight of a black and white animal. I thought at first that it was a groundhog as there were many of them around. As Cir ran to follow it, I realized in flash that it was a skunk and ran after them calling for Cir to come back. I caught up with Cir, just as he had stopped to determine what to do next, after the skunk had escaped under the neighbors' tent trailer. There was only a metre between them and the skunk was ready to spray when I grabbed Cir, ensuring that our stay in the cottage would not be interrupted prematurely.

As the leaves began to change color in the fall, radio stations began to promote weekend drives to see the fall colors. Because the forest in southern Ontario is mostly deciduous, the red and golden fall colors are spectacular. The trip we took with Vasek and Beatrice was rewarding as we saw not only the forest, which was a blaze of color, but also a unique feature of the area. There was a waterway which connected lakes and rivers with canals and a system of locks which allowed the water level to be changed, allowing the passage of boats. Built by early settlers in the area, the system is preserved as a park, the Trent-Severn Waterway.

At this time, Vasek was interested in buying another rural lot, closer to Toronto. We accompanied him several times as he drove out to inspect farms, buildings as well as surrounding forested areas. On one of these trips, we stopped to visit an old friend of Vasek's who owned a large tree farm. Some of his trees were now over a metre high and ready to be sold in the city. As he lived alone, we offered to help him and later also did some forest cleaning (cutting the overstory aspen to make more room for the conifers) for him. In return for this, we could take the dry trees for firewood and in the spring, he lent us a canoe so that we could try our skill on Lake Scugog.

When I mention firewood, I could not forget a lumberjack, who had heard that we were new residents at the cottage. One day he arrived, a tall, older man dressed in a checked shirt with a baseball cap (our exact image of a Canadian lumberjack), with a truckload of firewood which he offered, free of charge. I was glad that the neighbor came by to help me understand that we were not expected to pay for the wood. Vasek noted later that it was only advertising, so we would order from him next time, but I liked the gesture nonetheless.

When the trees finally shed their leaves, the children and I observed the flight of ducks and geese overhead, as we worked raking leaves and grass near the cottage. As we watched the birds we were struck by the variations in the hues of the sky. A friend in Czechoslovakia had once told us that the sky in Canada seemed to have a great many colors. Now we saw that he was right. When the sky was clear, it was more luminous than we had ever noted in Europe and the white clouds sometimes reminded me of whipping cream. Toward evening, purple and grey cloud would dominate the horizon. Maybe it was due to the flat country, but the sky was beautiful.

The end of November arrived and Petr began his five-month course, English as a Second Language. He found it difficult, as he had not made much effort before this to learn English. The language school in Toronto was perfect for newcomers, with students representing many different native languages. Students at the school were, after a short interview, placed in classes according to their knowledge of English. Each class ran for five to six weeks and ended with an exam. Those who passed the exam progressed to the next level. Petr began his studies at the first level and progressed through all five elementary classes. What surprised us was that some of the people registered in Petr's course had lived in Toronto for six, eight, and even fourteen years. How could they have lived, communicated with others, listened to radio, or watched television? Clearly, they must have lived in communities with others from the same country, so they did feel the ignorance of English to be such an obstacle. Personally, I found un-familiarity with the language spoken around me to be depressing and the only cure to spend as much time as possible in English lessons. It was discouraging at times. Though our knowledge increased as we studied, it seemed there was always more that we did not know and so we were always behind, trying to catch up.

During the winter, Beatrice and Vasek did not visit their cottage very much, so Petr often came alone. We usually started our shared week-ends by exchanging our impressions of what we were learning at school, poured out our problems, our despair over perceived failures, eventually concluding that we must and could endure it. We were certainly not the only ones who had gone through similar difficulties, and if others managed, why would we not. The second evening was dedicated to study. I remember writing about this to friends. "After one week of separation, we were finally together. Do you know what we did? We learned English!" I can recommend the study of another language to aging married couples who have difficulty finding common themes for discussion. If they take it as seriously as we did, they will surely find a lot to talk about.

Kate and Tom learned faster than we did, but their start was not easy either. The rural school was full, with thirty-two to thirty-eight children per classroom. There were no special education classes so their teachers had to find a way of communicating with our children during regular classes. I admired what they were able to accomplish without previous experience in teaching a second language and without any special texts to assist them or their students. On Tom and Kate's first day at school, the principal appealed to all the students to help the new students as much as they could, as they were from another country. Both of our children have good memories of how nice everyone in their first Canadian school was. The principal's public-address announcement also produced a translator. A girl of Kate's age reported that she could speak German, as her German-speaking parents maintained their first language at home, and she herself attended German school on Saturdays. The principal immediately put Kate in the same classroom and the girls sat together. Their teacher involved Kate as much as possible in the normal classroom work and she fit in quickly. Some years later, this teacher wrote to Kate that he had enjoyed the experience of teaching her so much that he was inspired to take special courses so that he could teach other foreign students.

Tom, being younger and having no-one to translate, felt lost at school. Unable to communicate though language, he tried to attract attention through inappropriate behavior. While the other children wrote or read, Tom would make faces to make them notice him and laugh. The final episode, where he had climbed on his desk to clown around, resulted in my being called to school for an interview. I was fortunate to have Beatrice with me, as she acted as both a translator and a psychologist. She understood and explained how Tom must feel in this school situation. We agreed on an increased workload for Tom, exactly what he needed to bring him to the point where he could fully join in the work of the class, and the problem behavior disappeared.

After school, Tom searched the neighborhood to find playmates. He was able to find several children living in the area and this also forced him to speak English. I permitted the children to watch one television program daily as this would also expose them to English. Of course, Kate and Tom loved this, and it did not take long before they imitated, "Scoo-be-doo, scoo-be-doo, where are you?"

Fall brought us two new holidays. Thanksgiving was the first, but as our friends did not celebrate it, we did not learn about this pleasant feast until the following year. Halloween was another matter. In the early evening on October 31, Helen called with excitement, "Tonight is Halloween. I will tell you the meaning later, but right now dress Kate and Tom in any costumes you can find and send them around to the neighbors' houses with the words 'trick or treat'." This was hard for me to understand but after several tries, I was able to repeat it and we followed her instructions. The only "costumes" we found were Vasek's old overalls and some clothes for gardening, but the children put together the assortment of long coats, big boots and hats full of holes and were soon dressed. Instead of flashlights, they carried candles to light their way. An hour later they returned, somewhat marked with wax drippings but very excited and happy. As we had no extra money to buy sweets, their "trick or treat" bags contained huge treasure. They had received not only candies, chocolate bars, cookies and chewing gum but also some money. None of us knew what kind of holiday this was, so the tales of houses decorated with pictures of witches, ghosts and jack o' lantern pumpkins were astonishing. They even told of one house where the access was illuminated by changing colorful lights and ghostly music could be heard. At another house they had seen a skeleton arm swinging over a handle.

Another positive outcome of Halloween was that the people in the area were introduced to the newcomers. A few days later, our closest neighbor came over explaining that someone had offered a bicycle for the children. What a joy! Kate claimed it, as it was a woman's bike. When Vasek saw what a source of pleasure this was, he took Petr to an auction in Toronto and they purchased an inexpensive bicycle for Tom.

As winter was quickly approaching, we were curious to find out whether the statements we had heard in Czechoslovakia about Canadian winters being really cold were true. We were quite aware that we were living in the southernmost part of the country. The reality was that temperatures did not drop below -30C but the high humidity and the open country with its large lakes, with little shelter from the wind, contributed to feeling quite cold. After the first heavy frost, Lake Scugog froze over. Never having lived near a lake like this, we did not trust the ice at first, but we soon learned from our neighbors that it was quite safe. Soon small booths resembling outhouses appeared on the lake. As we had never experienced ice fishing, this was all new to us and we were surprised to learn that many fishers used small stoves in their huts to keep warm. Snowmobiles were commonly used for transportation on the lake and some drove on the ice with their pickup trucks. People from all around the lake came together on this winter playground for children and adults, to fish, snowmobile, ski, skate and toboggan. We were tempted to purchase cross-country skiis, having enjoyed this sport in the past, but postponed doing so as we knew we would then have more belongings to move later. Our friends lent us an old pair of wooden skiis, so we could at least do solitary trips, though it was often so cold on the ice that we were glad to run back to the cottage.

It was in winter that we also met the parents of Stephanie, Kate's friend and translator at school. As this had been the first time that Stephanie could apply her knowledge of German, her parents were happy about the friendship. We also enjoyed the opportunity to converse in German again, though when I tried to switch back to English, I mixed the words from the two languages and sometimes could not remember expressions in either one. Stephanie's family lived on the other side of the lake, two kilometres over the ice or fifteen if we travelled around on the shore. When we visited on the weekends, we walked across the lake and they used their snowmobile.

Our new friendship had another benefit. Stephanie's father was a mechanic and owned a gas station, and he was willing to help us find a used car, as we could postpone purchasing a vehicle no longer. Vasek could not afford to lend Petr his car every weekend when they themselves were staying in Toronto. We decided to look for a truck, as this would give us more flexibility when the time came for us to move. Later we would put a camper on it, providing living and storage space for ourselves and our belongings. We found a suitable truck within two weeks, a twelve-year-old Dodge, with a cabin large enough for all of us and the dog. A friend of Petr's wrote to him soon after, asking if we already had a car and hoping we had bought a beautiful one. Well, the truck was reliable enough, but it had no beauty. Since the original owner was a farmer, we found grain hidden in the corners, even months later.

The next goal was obtaining drivers' licenses. Though we had held drivers' licenses for nearly twenty years they were valid here for only the first three months, so we had to pass exams to obtain Ontario drivers' licenses. English was again the main obstacle, especially when it came to idiomatic expressions. Finally, we managed it, after a second try for both of us. Petr had to write the theory portion twice and I had to be retested on driving. Parking was not a smooth operation with our big truck, and I was happy to accept our neighbor's offer to let me use her small car on my second try. The second driving test proceeded without any problems, so we both got our licenses, important personal documents, as we later learned.

12
First Christmas in Canada

"A life is beautiful and ideal or the reverse, only when we have taken into consideration the social as well as the family relationship." — Havelock Ellis

It was already close to Christmas, our first Christmas in Canada! The children looked forward to it and we adults joined them. At least for a while, we would have a break from school, a little bit of rest from daily stress. We would have more than a week together. Friends told us how busy Christmas time was, with parties and other events, but that was not yet our problem. Petr's only variation in routine course work was a discussion of the students' varied holiday customs during their final class before the Christmas break. My major new experience was the Christmas concert at Tom and Kate's school.

Stephanie's mother gave us a ride and helped me to get oriented in the school. This was my first time in a crowd of Canadian spectators, so I noticed how things differed from my previous experiences. I was surprised to see that young babies as well as toddlers were taken to the concert. The latter even had the privilege of sitting on a mattress placed close to the stage. In my old country, where extended families often live together, babies are usually left with their grandparents when parents attend public events. I noticed every kind of dress, from evening wear with lace to jeans and t-shirts. Spectators arrived late and left early, but nobody warned them or seemed to care. The concert had been well rehearsed, but it was a long one. Each classroom gave presentations of songs, recitations or plays, and there were a lot of classrooms in the school. Of course all the parents wanted to see their children, and I was no exception. I was happy that Tom and Kate were able to join their Canadian classmates in performing. Tom acted in a short play. Kate was proud to have been chosen to play the recorder with a few of her classmates while the rest sang. They had only begun learning their instruments a little before the concert.

At the cottage, we could prepare for Christmas as we used to do. We baked cookies and remembered how much we had missed this important aspect of our celebrations last year. The children secretly prepared their gifts and we wondered how much money we could afford to spend. Following customs from Czechoslovakia, Kate and Tom each wrote a letter to the Christ-child, as Santa Claus is not part of our traditions. Kate wished for a big doll, Tom for a bulldozer for outdoor play. These wishes could be fulfilled. A walk in the nearby forest yielded a small Douglas fir which would serve for our Christmas tree.

Our holiday was pleasant and peaceful. Beatrice and Vasek had decided to stay in Toronto, so we celebrated with just our circle of family. They invited us to join them in Toronto, but having just finished our driving exams, we decided not to go and kept our visiting closer to home. Stephanie's parents had invited us for Boxing Day supper and we also visited and exchanged gifts with our friends in Lindsay. They invited us to spend New Year's eve with them at their timeshare condo by Lake Simcoe. This was our first experience of this kind of holiday, where people pay for a few weeks' use of a condo which is used the rest of the time by other owners. We liked this idea in contrast to the usual type of cottage ownership which leaves the cottages, which take up so much space, empty most of the time. Unfortunately, it was so cold that we had to change our plans for outdoor activities to using the indoor swimming pool. We found it pleasant to enjoy the warmth of the pool and the view of the snow-covered countryside through the big windows partly shaded by the lush palms planted around the pool.

Our toast to a "successful New Year" was a little hesitant as we prepared to resume our everyday life, a life which seemed to revolve around studying English. The uncertainty of what we would do after our language courses were completed now began to occupy our thoughts. As we began this New Year, we did not know where we would celebrate the next one. Though we told ourselves that we had taken the most important step, to reach Canada, we knew that many other steps would soon follow.

Petr's courses finished in May, but we wanted to stay where we were until the children finished their school year. In the meantime, we needed to find jobs somewhere, though it seemed that this did not look promising. We found, to our surprise, that while people around us were friendly and helpful in many small ways, not many had leads for finding work. We were invited to one gathering where the question, "What to do as newcomers?" produced the answer, "Raise earthworms!" Nobody had thought of the practical considerations such as start-up money and not having a place of our own or any idea of how to do business in an unfamiliar environment. Afterwards, one lady told me sincerely, "You know, it is nice to dream a little bit, especially if it is not my problem." I thanked her for her concern, though there was no help for us there.

More helpful, was advice to write resumés and send them to every place that might be interested in our training and experience. First, we had to find addresses, a larger task than we expected. We sent letters and resumés to government forest offices, large companies with pulpmills and sawmills, even provincial and national parks. I know today, that this approach was hopeless. Nobody treats such correspondence seriously unless the person is applying for an advertised position. Parks offices, especially, receive so much mail that they could not possibly answer it all. I mailed about eighty applications for each of us. Not having a computer, I produced them all on a borrowed typewriter, in the best English I could in those days. Later a friend made so many corrections to what I had written that it all seemed completely changed. So, unfortunately, the results of all this work were poor. Only about ten percent of employers answered at all, whether that answer was a "no, thank you" or "we will put your application on file." Of course, I learned later that this did not mean anything — our qualifications in forestry were good, we simply did not have any idea of how and where to apply for work.

Finally, it was not my letters, but a friend that gave us hope. Petr knew this man from Czechoslovakia, where he and Petr had both been involved in the kennel organization. He was an internationally respected zoologist and mostly worked in research, even after his escape from his country of origin. After several moves, this man, also a talented painter who had exhibited work in many galleries, had come to the Toronto area. I could not believe that he would be willing to help us — but he was! He and his wife invited us for a visit and as we discussed our problem after lunch, he remembered a Finnish friend in northwestern Ontario who was building a sawmill. Our friend contacted him and we also wrote a letter. We did not know it then, but our timing coincided with the nearly finished sawmill burning to the ground, so we waited, all spring, anxiously and in vain for any reply, as travel to north-western Ontario at this time, just for an answer, was not possible.

We continued with schooling and English study, with the children making the greatest improvements. Even Petr and I communicated much better than we had on our arrival, talking with our neighbors and making the switch from German to English conversation with Stephanie's parents. It was another pleasure to be able to finally understand the words on the country-music tapes which we had brought with us from Czechoslovakia.

We found that Canadian schools had fewer holiday breaks than German schools, as there were no more until spring break in March. Tom's birthday fell at the same time and Vasek and Beatrice invited us all to Toronto to spend the week visiting city attractions as well as celebrating the birthday with them. These are now some of our best memories of Toronto. Despite the grey weather, the human relationships that truly determine the atmosphere gave us a week of "sunshine." Beatrice prepared a festive birthday dinner and Vasek acted as our cheerful tour guide during our days of sightseeing. Only Petr had no holidays.

Many new attractions had opened for the school holiday. The most tempting was the exhibition of dinosaurs at the city museum. In addition to the displays, there were film showings and contests for children of all ages. I could not believe my eyes when museum staff showed artifacts and actually allow them to circulate among the children. I had been brought up not to touch anything in a museum and viewed artifacts as dead stuff. Now my children were excited and enthusiastic as the story of dinosaurs came to life for them. We also saw displays of Egyptian art and of the Canadian Group of Seven painters, which were new to me. Petr was able to come with us to the Science Museum and we noticed again that the exhibitions were attractive to children of all ages. They could test their strength, endurance, and dexterity. One display allowed them to pedal a bicycle and lift a small ball using this momentum — as they pedalled faster, the ball was lifted higher. Each room was devoted to specific branches of science and movies were shown to complement the displays. Despite spending the entire day there, Tom and Kate were not tired but enthusiastic to see more.

Our walks in the city led to the CN Tower, Chinatown and Lake Erie. I even did some window shopping with Beatrice. Unexpectedly, we were invited to visit another Czech family. The husband had studied, through correspondence, at the same forestry school as I. Their children were the same ages as Tom and Kate and, to our surprise, the children spoke together in English and not in Czech!

The first sign of spring at the cottage was the change in the lake. First, the fishing huts gradually disappeared, then the snowmobiles. It was mid-April when we set out to cross the lake on the ice to visit Stephanie's family, surprised that in spite of the sunny weather, we did not meet anyone. Then, suddenly in the middle of the lake we came upon open water with ducks and geese on it. My early fears about the ice returned and I forced my family to make a long detour. When Stephanie's parents found out about our crossing, they nearly scolded us for doing something so dangerous. They insisted on driving us back when it was time to go home. We did not cross on the ice again and within a couple of weeks, it broke and melted completely.

I have always enjoyed spring in the country. As the first flowers in the garden and the nearby forest poked out their heads, I did not know which I admired more. The trillium, the provincial flower of Ontario, with both white and purple blooms, was probably my favorite. I also found primroses, anemones and several kinds of daisies on my walks. Hundreds of tulips grew in Vasek's garden, and when they were all in bloom, the sight was unforgetable. Gardening began again, with Vasek and Beatrice coming to the cottage often. We helped to plant vegetables and flowers and dug out some trees for replanting. One Sunday afternoon, Vasek went down to the lower part of the lot, near the lake, to dig more trees and found Tom literally standing among snakes. They were harmless green snakes but it was still very strange to see him there. Their length varied from fifty centimetres to a metre and they were in the process of moving from tree to tree. When Tom had stepped between two of the trees, they used him as a bridge. The whole show lasted about an hour and it was hard to find a single snake afterwards.

Another experience we had that spring concerned the adoption of a young robin. Unable to fly yet, it sat on the lawn, apparently lost, one cool day. When a cat came by, we decided to move the bird inside, where it soon recovered. We now had the task of supplying it with fresh worms each day and the children even took it to school one day, to the delight of their classmates. The week after this, Petr found a nest with four young in it, almost at the point of trying their wings. Early the next morning, he added "our" robin to the nest. A day later, the young robins learned to fly and a few days after this, I witnessed an oddly touching scene. There were the parent birds, feeding five young robins, all perched in a row. The adoption process was complete.

Also early that spring, Cir and a neighbor's dog teamed up to kill a young porcupine. How it happened, I did not know, as I only found a piece of porcupine skin in front of Cir's doghouse. We knew that he could not be the main actor, as he got only two quills. The neighbor's dog had picked up almost thirty and we had to use pliers to get them out, accompanied by the dog's heartbreaking cries. Cir, unfortunately, got the idea that catching porcupines was an easy business and had to pay dearly for it with his own pain until he finally quit chasing them.

Just before Easter, and with help from Stephanie's father, we bought a camper to fit on our truck. Previously owned by a farmer and used only for a few hunting trips, it was comfortably equipped with a heater, stove, fridge and upper and lower bunks which converted to benches around a table for day use. We had never seen anything like this in Europe and set off for Algonquin Park to try it out. The problem was that though spring had arrived in southern Ontario, the park was still snow-covered and the lakes were frozen. The only creatures we encountered were grouse and white-tailed deer, but we found the natural beauty and solitude very pleasant. As night came, and with it colder temperatures, we discovered that the heater did not work. However, we got some warmth from the burners of the stove and stayed until Easter Sunday. Unfortunately, our truck had a big appetite for gas, especially with the camper on. On the way back, we ran out of gas. All the gas stations we had passed were closed. It took a while to find some people who were willing to drive us to the next open gas station and back to our truck, so we could continue.

As spring wore on, Petr looked more and more unhappy each time he arrived at the cottage. His course was finishing and the strain of living as a house guest for almost a full year was becoming too much for him and our friends. We were grateful for their sponsorship and much obliged to them for sharing their home and cottage so generously, but we were stressed from coping with school, searching for work, and the insecurity we felt. Even small problems irritated us and grew bigger. As we waited for word from the sawmill, we realized that this was our third spring of living in uncertainty about our future. We did not want to feel that we were a burden any longer and decided to ask at school if the children could finish two weeks early. We would set off, north-west to the sawmill, looking for work along the way. We had names and addresses, supplied through our contacts with the Czech organization, of people along the way who might help us with our job search. Even the act of making a plan lifted our spirits a great deal.

Then, about a week before our scheduled departure, a short letter from the sawmill arrived. The owner wanted to know when Petr could start because he had a "nice job" for him. It was wonderful news! Of course we were curious about what a "nice job" would be, but it did not matter. What mattered most was that we had hope as we set off on our journey.

13
A Job in North-western Ontario

"Generations of great thinkers have dreamed of a moneyless society somewhere in the future. As far as my family is concerned, we're already ahead of our time." — author unkown

Petr was the first to finish school. I was the second, as I stopped driving to Lindsay before the exams. Some teachers did not understand why I did not take the final exams, but I had attended classes to improve my English and not to gain knowledge of the high school subject material. We had not yet mastered the English language but we definitely knew enough to communicate. Our children completed their school year very well. It was nearly the same as in Germany — within a year they could speak fluently. However, they were, just as quickly, losing their ability to speak their other languages. At home, we had to start speaking only in Czech; otherwise Kate and Tom would forget, as they did with German.

Meanwhile, we managed to make a short trip to Midland, which had a memorial to the first Catholic missionaries in Canada.Then we started to say "Good-bye" to our friends. I guess Vasek and Beatrice relaxed when they saw that we would depart soon, so our time together was enjoyable. With them and other friends from Lindsay, we had a pleasant supper on the deck of the cottage one warm pre-summer evening. Beatrice expressed her regrets for us. She felt as we were leaving for the north, we would miss the warm summer weather. At this time, we did not have any idea about weather elsewhere in Canada. We only hoped for some summer there and said that if other people could manage, why not us? If only we had known, just how hot weather could be where we were going!

All our belongings were easy to store in the camper and we still had enough room to move around. We even took Kate and Tom's bicycles. I remember a saying: "All things I carry with me." In our case it was modified: "All things we drive with us," which was completely true. On a beautiful sunny morning, still full of dew, that promised a warm day, we said farewell to our sponsors, thanked them again, and took some last pictures. In fact, these were the first pictures of our trip. And we set off! We were equipped with maps and information so we would know the way ahead. The day was beautiful, the trip was wonderful, but the best of all was our mood. We were just soaring with enthusiasm and happiness, not only because we would see another part of Canada, as the trip to Ignace was about 1800 km, but mostly because we finally felt free. We did not need to obey any instructions, where to go, what to do. It depended completely on us, what to do for the next days. After nearly two years of unconscious fearfulness, the feeling of freedom was so strong, I hardly can compare it to anything else in our lives.

I know careful people would do many things differently. We were obligated to stay with our sponsor for twelve months, but we left after ten months. We had no life insurance, as we did not have the money for it. We heard in Lindsay that there was a chance that our children would be returned to Czechoslovakia if something happened to us. Unfortunately, we did not have any close friends willing to be their guardians — so we chose not think about it. We preferred to smile and to enjoy the present time, than to worry!

During the first day we drove close to Lake Huron. The land is, unfortunately, mostly private and fenced, so we had only an occasional glimpse of the lake's blue water and the many islands near the shore. After a while, the farmland changed to deciduous forest which accompanied us until the northern part of Lake Superior. The first night we parked in a campground by Sault Ste. Marie, on a headland where the waters of the two big lakes mix. Only a narrow strip of land separated us from Lake Michigan. So we were in close proximity to three Great Lakes! The fourth, Lake Ontario, we had already seen in Toronto.

I have a personal feeling for Lake Superior. In the Czech language, the translation of "Superior" is the same as my birth name. When we learned about the Great Lakes at school in Czechoslovakia, my schoolmates laughed, saying that I had a lake in Canada. Over the years of growing up, I had slowly abandoned my dreams to travel and see this lake. Now, suddenly, I was camped with my family on its shore. When I saw the clear water I could not believe the feeling that came over me! I knew our journey here came at a high price: we had lost our families, friends, positions, and belongings. Even in the future, we would continue to pay the price, but for this moment, it was all worth while.

It was easy to live in our camper: to cook supper, to read a book with the children, and to sleep there at night. On this trip we found an excellent system of campgrounds equipped with showers, washrooms, and firewood. The fees were reasonable, even for us.

As we left the campground in the morning, we noticed the white flowers of bunchberries which filled every corner. Later, driving along the shore of Lake Superior, we could not resist stopping to take pictures. The water was crystal clear. We saw huge boulders several metres below the surface. Our dog, Cir, was confused by the clear water and wanted to jump from one boulder to the another, only to be submerged in the freezing water. How vigorously he shook it out!

Finally, the coniferous forest, in the form of the narrow black spruce, appeared. Unfortunately, a little more to the north we ran into fog, so we mostly guessed at the road, than actually saw it. One of the addresses for "may be helpful," which we got in Toronto, was located close to Lake Nipigon. We made a detour to the place but, unfortunately, no one was home and there was nothing to indicate a speedy return of the inhabitants. As we wanted to see Thunder Bay and the road to Ignace in full light, we stopped early to camp. Mosquitos interrupted our ball game and forced us to find refuge in the camper. The next morning was again beautiful, without any fog or mosquitos. We drove through Thunder Bay, which is dominated by a hill and well-known as a ski centre. Otherwise, we did not find the city very interesting, as it was like most cities in North America. It was only at the port that we walked for a while and watched the big inland ferry ships and fishing boats. I was shocked when I saw big lake trout being taken from Superior. According to "common knowledge" in Europe, the Great Lakes are nearly "dead," with no fish. Now I saw that it was not true. Fishermen were still catching fish here, but much fewer than years ago. On the edge of the city, I was captivated by a view of a bulldozer turning the soil. The ground was covered with marsh-loving flowers — Labrador tea and purple laurel. It was the first time this soil had been turned, not as in Europe, where the soil has been turned nearly everywhere, literally a thousand times.

Beyond Thunder Bay, we visited Kakabeka Falls which had an attractive new access. Afterwards, we drove through gently rolling country, with no outstanding landmarks except the many lakes. The forest was mostly coniferous and the prevalent species was jack pine with only scattered islands of the taller white or red pine. Black spruce grew in the marshy places. Aspen and poplar are the only two species which grow in the deciduous forests far to the north and west to Alberta. A couple of years later, we finally saw forests of other deciduous species in British Columbia.

Both Petr and I were a little bit nervous on the last part of our trip and repeatedly discussed and thought about what we could expect in the near future. Driving from Thunder Bay to the west, we saw only small hamlets, usually centred around gas stations. Ignace was the first town, 250 kilometres west of the city, so it was impossible to miss. The Trans Canada Highway went directly through the town and cut it in half. At that time, the town had a population of about 2500 people. As we found later, most of the people worked in mining or in the forest industry. Other income came from recreation, as the place was famous for good fishing. In the fall, many hunters came for moose, deer or black bear.

On arrival, we investigated the part of town close to the highway. We found where to buy groceries and, above all, we got information on how to get to the sawmill. It was located ten kilometres further to the west. We again passed several lakes and when we finally turned off the main road to the sawmill, we found that it was built directly on the shore of a big lake. The camp itself, where there was accommodation for the workers and a kitchen, was about one kilometre from the mill, on the shore of a smaller lake. To our regret, Mr. Kanes was not there but they did expect him back late the same day or next morning. We were not sure if we could stay in the camp, so we decided on a compromise. We drove back to the intersection between the sawmill and the camp and prepared to camp there. I began to make our supper while Petr, Kate and Tom played ball. Suddenly, a friendly bitch joined our dog. Soon her master appeared and, surprised to see us, asked what we were doing there. She was the sawmill owner's wife, and had not yet heard about our arrival. When we explained, she was friendly and invited us to move to the camp, where we would have access to water, outhouses and a sauna. She accompanied us for a closer look it.

It was only a small mobile camp, consisting of six small trailers and a large one, which housed the kitchen and dining room. There was no hook-up to electric power, so stoves, lights, and even refrigerators used propane. The small trailers had oil stoves — of course they were not in use now. Northern days were longer than we were used to in the south and we soon found how hot they can be. Water from the lake was used for washing and drinking water came from a well. I believe it all came from the same source with the only difference being that the well water was filtered through the sand. During the warm summer days, the only place where they used firewood was in the sauna. As the camp did not have any other bathing facilities, the sauna was heavily used. It was built directly on the shore, so everybody who liked a fast cool-down could jump directly into the lake. The owner and most of his workers were originally from Finland. Clearly, the landscape with its many lakes reminded them of their homeland. The sauna was surely a natural part of their lifestyle. Just in front of the sauna, a small plane rocked on the lake. The owner used it for guiding hunters in the fall and in his lumbering business, as the country was flat and hard to survey from the ground. It was much easier to use a plane with floats because then it could land on any of the numerous lakes.

The next day, when Mr. Kanes arrived, he agreed to hire Petr immediately. The job offer was a good one. Petr would be a supervisor of three to four groups of forest workers who would supply the sawmill with timber. However, that was only a prospect for the future. Presently, the sawmill was in the midst of reconstruction because of the fire in the winter. Every effort was being made to finish it soon and to begin operating. So Petr started out by working on construction. All twelve to fifteen workers boarded in the kitchen. To save money, we decided that Petr would eat with us. Mrs. Kanes cooked for the whole camp but she hired only occasional help from Ignace when the number of workers increased. The next day, when I stopped by the kitchen, she asked me if I would like to help her. I happily agreed, glad I could still supervise our children and add $25 a day to our budget.

The day after our arrival, the sawmill owner took us for a ride. We went to the forest, where he planned to do some logging, and around the closest lakes. It was a strange country for us, but had its own charm. We understood why the Finns felt at home in this land with its gently rolling, forested terrain and many lakes. Some of these were connected by creeks and brooks, others surrounded by swamps. The latter type was a source of two problems for us. First, it was impossible to walk very far in this country. Trails usually finished beside a lake or in a swamp and our stroll was quickly over. Secondly, all the stagnant water was an ideal habitat for mosquitos and other insects, such as black flies and deer flies. It took a while to adjust, as we always had to dress with long sleeves and pants when we went into the forest. Even then we still got some bites. Later, we heard that the bumps behind one's ears are some kind of proof that one is an outdoorsman.

Petr and I tried to find a place to rent in Ignace. Unfortunately, we found that the town was fully occupied in summer, as vacant rooms and houses were rented to tourists. The sawmill owner made us an offer to stay in the camp and use a small one-room trailer, two and a half by five metres in size. Finally, we had to agree. Just beside the trailer we arranged our camper to serve as a kitchen, equipping it with a stove and a fridge. We all slept in the back of the trailer and set up a table and chairs in the front part. However, we spent most of our time outside as the days were warm, even hot. With a smile, I often remembered how Beatrice had expressed her regret that we were going to spend our summer in the cool north.

There was plenty of work and after a while the days took on a repetitive pattern. In the morning, I got up first and hastened to the main kitchen to prepare and serve breakfast. Petr, with Kate and Tom, prepared their meal themselves. After breakfast, I went back to the trailer to check on our children and to plan the day. Then it was back to the kitchen to wash dishes and prepare lunch. When everything was ready, about 11:00 a.m., I would run to my "kitchen" to do lunch for us. Afterwards, dishes awaited me in both places, but Kate and Tom helped in our place. In the afternoon, we sometimes went with Mrs. Kanes to town to do laundry or shopping. Then it was time to prepare supper for the work crew. In between, I had a little spare time to start our supper and prepare the sauna. When I finished supper in the "big" kitchen, that left the dishes and clean up. The next day the cycle repeated. I had never done this kind of job, but I liked cooking and baking, so that came in handy now. Weekends meant I was mostly off duty (in the "big" kitchen, not in my own). Many workers were from Thunder Bay and went home for the weekend. However, when the construction of the sawmill was almost finished, nearly everybody worked overtime and on weekends, so the kitchen ran for seven days a week.

At the start of my work, I was a little worried about our children, but when I saw that everything went smoothly, I was glad. They were not likely to go far from the camp — just to the sawmill, lakes, and the forest nearby. Both children had their chores, but otherwise they were free to enjoy the beautiful summer outdoors. Their favorite activities were swimming and canoeing. The lakes here were mostly shallow with sandy beaches and bottoms. In the lake by the sawmill one could go more than 500 metres from the shore and still be only knee-deep in water. Both children were good swimmers, so after we set some rules, I left them free to splash. They had both learned a little about canoeing at Lake Squgog, but here they used a safer, aluminium canoe. The lakes here were also safer, rough water was rare, so Kate and Tom took longer trips. I will never forget the day I saw, from the main kitchen window, an approaching passengerless canoe, which leaned to one side. I could not see Tom's head bobbing behind. He had leaned over too much, tipping into the water. He was not able to pour the water out, so he swam behind the canoe and pushed it to the shore. Another memory of this time concerned Kate, who had learned to play a recorder when we lived in Lindsay. She liked it very much, so she practised over the summer. Once Mrs. Kanes saw Kate, sitting among the jack pines, her music scattered around her, deep in concentration as she played. Mrs. Kanes was so touched by the scene that she told everybody about it.

This was a description, taken from my journal, of a day in the camp: "The mornings are cooler, but not too much. There is a fog above the lake, but that will disappear about 8:00 a.m. and another beautiful day will begin. From the kitchen window I see, through the jack pines, the lake and how its water makes ripples and mirrors the sunshine back to our window. The plane lightly rocks on the surface. Sometimes the water is smooth as glass — mostly in the evenings, never in the mornings. Loons call. First, there were three, now there are seven. We see them all day, but they call only in the mornings and evenings. Sometimes we see rings on the lake's surface, where a fish has jumped. Dragonflies murmur and grasshoppers twitter on the sand. A family of swallows had a nest by the kitchen door. The parents attacked everybody who went in or out. The young have now left the nest and it is silent. Occasionally we hear the sound of a heavy truck from the highway or a train. Before it rains or when the temperature is cooler, the kitchen door and window netting are busy with mosquitoes. Their buzzing suggests what we can expect outside."

As I mentioned, this place was paradise for everybody who liked water, especially for fishermen and canoeists. A canoe is really the best transportation in a true wilderness. Most local roads were for access to logging areas, so travel by road was not attractive. In contrast, waterways gave unrestricted possibilities, especially if the travellers were willing to portage when needed. We met several people who journeyed on the lakes and rivers through a large area in northern Ontario. We found out later that there was a famous route leading from Ignace south through several lakes and portages. On this route, an eccentric man had built a large house having several floors. He lived alone until he met his death in the closest lake. Later, when we bought our own canoe, we planned to make this trip. Unfortunately it did not happen, but we made many other trips. Often we were lucky enough to see wild animals from the canoe. Because the camp was some distance from the nearest town, we felt that the wilderness was just a reach of the hand away. The lakes around us were full of different species of ducks as well as the aforementioned loons. Flocks of grouse lived just around the camp. When the blueberries were ripe, grouse would come into camp despite people or dogs. Cir sometimes could not resist trying to catch them. It was useless, they just fled a little further. A couple of times, they even landed directly on him. Both dogs were, in fact, more upset with the squirrels. They chattered agitatedly and sometimes imprudently skipped just in front of the dogs' noses. It was often too much, even for the most peaceful dog. The "homo sapiens" inhabitants too were likely to lose patience with the squirrels — for instance, when they promenaded on the laundry line, where we had hung freshly washed clothes. Squirrels did not hesitate to throw laundry pins, to bite lines or even the clothes. They also had a fancy to collect toilet paper. In the outhouses, we had to cover the rolls with plastic pails. It was always a surprise to open the outhouse door and have a squirrel swiftly jump against it. If this happened at night, the unlucky one was shocked fully awake.

There were also many beavers around. The closest beaver lodge was next to the "camp" lake. We often heard it in camp when the beavers slapped water with their tails. The sound was like a gunshot. We spent hours watching them despite the mosquito bites. Several times, we saw deer and moose around the camp. In the time of moose rut, one cow brought her suitor to the "camp" lake. She grazed on water plants with her head deep in the water while her mate just watched her. When she lifted her head, the water plants were wrapped around her neck like garlands. Neither animal paid any attention to us. Only once did we see a black bear close the camp. We saw many others out in the bush, but they did not bother us in camp. Once we experienced a visit which could have cost Cir his life. It was already November, the lakes were frozen and we were living in Ignace. We had come out one evening to take a sauna. Cir ran outside with the owner's bitch which had been left alone in the camp. Everybody else had gone to Thunder Bay. As we sat comfortably in the hot sauna, we saw the dogs running and barking on the frozen lake, in the full moonlight. Suddenly, we heard yelping and when we looked again, we saw both dogs running back for dear life. At their heels ran a pack of five wolves. The wolves were very close, running side by side and trying to separate the dogs. There was no time for us to dress and run to help. The only thing that we could do was to run naked outside and scream. We took along a kerosene light, and in an effort to increase the noise, we drummed on the sauna door. The dogs instinctively ran toward us. It helped! Our appearance and the noise discouraged the wolves and they just disappeared. I don't need to mention that, afterwards, the dogs kept close the sauna.

Another thing we always recall about Ignace is the abundance of mushrooms and berries. On our very first day, I found excellent mushrooms growing on the sandy soil. Back in south Ontario, we would occasionally find good mushrooms, but here they grew everywhere: in the camp, along the roads, in the bush. They could be found from June until the first frost in September and in quantity. I have always liked to pick mushrooms, and my European attitude was to gather all I found. But it was impossible — what to do with them? I dried some for winter use but I had to learn to ignore them and pick just a few when I needed them for cooking. I did not know yet that mushroom picking was not popular in Canada. On the contrary, people here were afraid to even taste any wild mushrooms for fear that they might be poisonous. When I first showed my enthusiasm for mushrooms in front of Mrs. Kanes, she gave me a suspicious look. Two days later, she invited us for supper and admitted that she thought we did not have enough money for decent food, so we ate mushrooms. Even later, she would never try them and always bought mushrooms at the store. It was different with berries. First, we picked some wild strawberries around the camp. There were not many, just enough to make dessert and a little jam. When Mrs. Kanes saw how I liked the picking and that both children helped, she planned a trip to gather blueberries. She told us that she knew places where blueberries grew in abundance. These places were originally huge areas of forest where a fire had rampaged three or four years ago. The only problem was the bumpy logging roads. We had never experienced such quantities of blueberries: within an hour, each of us had filled a four-litre bucket! Because we made such trips on weekends, Petr was also with us. One weekend, we collected 160 litres! I personally gave up one Sunday and went to pick some raspberries by the side of a road. Afterwards, we had the challenge of finding what to do with so many berries. Of course, I preserved some and a share also went to the "big" kitchen. However, we still had many bags of berries. Finally, our friends from Ignace offered us some space in their freezer on the condition that we take them all back before the fall hunting season. We eventually bought our own freezer in Thunder Bay.

With the opening of hunting season, our friends from Toronto, who had helped Petr to find this job, came to hunt moose: in fact, two moose, as both the friend and his wife had tags. Both were successful and each got a moose. However, they had to move them to a place accessible to their car. Petr was called on to help with the heavy task. First, they had to clean both moose, cut them into transportable pieces, and then Petr carried these to the closest lake. At the lake they had to load the meat into a canoe, and then from the canoe into Mr. Kanes's plane. The weight overloaded the plane, so it could not leave the water. That meant they had to load part of it back into the canoe and make another trip to the cottage where our friends were staying. After all the meat had been cleaned, packed in ice, and loaded into their small trailer, the hunters had to drive home immediately instead of taking a well-earned rest, so the meat would not spoil in the suddenly warm October weather. Nor were they able to take all the meat with them, there was enough to give some to the sawmill owners and some to us. Of course, we were overjoyed. We were taking a hunting course (again we encountered so many new words!), but we had not been able to get a hunting permit on time. In exchange for the meat, I gave our friends some of my blueberries, a very good deal for us, as we laughed about it later.

The culture of the hunt in Canada was new for us, especially the idea of hunting for meat, not just for trophies as we knew from Europe. Often we saw a good moose rack set somewhere in a yard, as the hunter did not prize it. On the other hand, he could tell us how many hamburgers and steaks he made from each moose. Some evenings, in hunting season, when we drove through Ignace it reminded us of

Europe in fall when people would slaughter their pigs. Instead of pigs, moose would be hanging in lighted garages while the happy hunter, with family and friends, worked on it.

It was already around Thanksgiving when suddenly warm weather came again. Just before the holiday, we picked the last berries — bog cranberries. Their leaves already fallen due to September's frost, the appearance of the plants against the moss made me think of red beads on a green carpet. We found enough to make sauce for a traditional Thanksgiving turkey and had some left for Christmas. I liked the Thanksgiving holiday very much. It reminded me of similar feasts in Czech villages, where they also gave thanks for a good crop.

We spent this holiday in a cottage, where we had been a couple of times in the summer. On our first visit, we experienced an unbelievable display of fireflies. They looked as dazzling as small moving fires. On another visit, Mrs. Kanes introduced us to a lady trapper. She had lived there nearly thirty years. Her place was now accessible by car, but she remembered a time, when she had to go shopping to Ignace by canoe in summer and by dog-sled in winter. The trip then took her from two to four hours. On our next visit, we found her and her boyfriend drunk as pigs. I started to think that probably only strong characters can live so remotely. It seemed to me that this couple did not in any way refine the nature of the place around them, and the wild place definitely did not refine them.

It was already fall when we moved to Ignace. We experienced a little stress looking for a place to rent as our children had already started school. The school bus would pick Kate and Tom up on the highway at the turn-off to the sawmill. They rode their bicycles between camp and the intersection. At the beginning of September, the weather cooled down and the first snow fell, so I had to pull out the warm clothing, including toques and mittens. We had to start heating our small trailer and the single windows fogged up. There was not enough room at the kitchen table for both children to do their homework. It was definitely time to move. Following advice from our friends, we were, for a while, thinking of buying a house. However, when we learned how the interest rates worked and found that we did not have enough for a down payment, we abandoned that idea. Later, we were glad of our decision. Finally Randy, Petr's friend from the sawmill found us a place to rent. As we hesitantly looked at some advertisements in Ignace, Randy came along. He took charge: driving through the town, within half an hour, he had found a place for us. It was a trailer, but this one had two bedrooms and a built-on addition. Inside, there was, in our view, the best equipment a trailer could have — a wood stove. We found out later that the trailer had come from somewhere in the south as it had minimal insulation. The walls in the master bedroom, which was located in the very back, were frozen through and we often had to tear our clothing away where the frost would make it stick. Fortunately, due to the wood stove, we survived even the severe frost. The house was separated by a fence from an auto wrecker's place, as our landlord ran a garage service. Before us, some bachelor mechanics had lived in the trailer and I had a hard time cleaning it up to our standards. It was about 200 metres to the nearest neighbor, so there was enough room for Cir. The trailer had some furniture, and we borrowed some benches and a table from the sawmill. Petr made beds and some shelves. He also built a small workshop and a shelter for firewood. We contemplated how many times we had built improvements to our living space to meet our needs, only to move again.

Meanwhile, the sawmill reopened and everything looked good. I drove there with Petr, but went back before supper, so I did not help with serving the meal or cleaning afterward. At the same time, a very tempting opportunity came up in Ignace. Through an educational institute, the town offered English as a Second Language. There were many French miners, who came from Quebec to work in Ignace, and often their wives applied for this course. When I found I could even get an allowance, which was nearly equal to my wage in the kitchen, I decided to apply also. I did not feel right about quitting at the sawmill, however. I did not know yet, this was normal. People move from place to place because of better jobs and they are do not attach strongly to one location. Once we read a statistic which surprised us: the average family moves once every three to five years! Later, we witnessed for ourselves how people moved from one province to another, depending on economic opportunity. They did not have bonds to their houses, or sometimes even to their families and friends, as we knew to be the norm in Europe. Often we heard stories of how families lost touch with their members and then tried to find them through advertisements. We also heard how, for many years, even decades, some people did not see their parents, children, or other family members. Even in a country as large as Canada, it sounded unbelievable to us when we viewed it through the lens of our experience.

The English course was the best I could get in Ignace. Of course it was not as intensive or on the level of Petr's course in Toronto. However, I learned a lot. There were twelve students and a teacher from the local high school. She later admitted that she did not have enough course materials in the beginning, so she had to create her own plan for each day. Yet it was great! The necessity of daily listening, speaking, reading, and learning new words gave me the courage to initiate conversations myself, not just to answer when somebody asked me a question. I had another advantage here. My eleven classmates talked occasionally among themselves in French, so my teacher, Anne, and I talked together in English.This gave me an opportunity for extra practice. The other great thing for me was the discovery of the many materials available in a library. We went to the local library at the start of our course and then repeatedly afterwards. I had already noticed in Lindsay how well equipped the libraries were and my experience in Ignace confirmed it. In the beginning, I only borrowed magazines, but Anne encouraged me to read more than articles and to take, at least, simple books. We also worked in class with books and wrote short summaries. To my surprise, after a while, I began to read more quickly and used a dictionary only occasionally. Reading was, for me, somehow easier than speaking.

One Sunday afternoon, an explosion shook the town. My first thought was that a helicopter had crashed in our neighborhood. When we ran out of the house, we saw flames on the opposite side. Maybe, we thought, the gas station had exploded. Later we heard that one of the lines of a three-line gas pipeline, which runs from Alaska to Ontario, through Ignace, had exploded. The fire, which looked so close, was actually two kilometres from the town. Luckily, because of the snow, the fire did not spread far. However, the thunderous explosion and the flames scared many citizens. When we talked about it at school, our teacher admitted that she grabbed her purse, which she considered in this moment, her most important possession, and was ready to flee out of town. In fact, many people did leave town, only to return a couple of hours later. I look back now in amusement at how we, the students, tried to describe our alarm in spite of our restricted word supply.

The school was located beside a major mall, about a kilometre and a half from our house. As Petr used the truck for transportation to the sawmill, I walked the distance to the school. I liked the walk but when the temperature fell below -40°C, I arrived at the classroom so cold, I was unable to even speak. When my schoolmates found out that I didn't have any transportation, somebody always came to give me ride on cold days after this. The best result of our classes was that after a couple of months we were able to talk together in English. Some of my classmates were so encouraged by their progress that they settled permanently in Ignace.

Petr and I were not so enthusiastic about Ignace. When the summer was over, we felt a little isolated, lonely. I don't think it was due to the location of the town, on the Trans Canada Highway but far from other towns. As I mentioned, to the east it was 250 kilometres to Thunder Bay, to the west — 100 kilometres to Dryden, which had a population of 6500. Back in Czechoslovakia, we also lived in isolation, in a hamlet with only five houses. However, we were visited by friends and families, so we were seldom alone for weekends. We made trips to the mountains, went cross-country skiing and horse-back riding, and engaged in many other activities as a part of our daily lives. Now, we did not have many friends and we could not spend much time outdoors because of cold weather. And we knew we missed the mountains. The landscape around Ignace had its own charm, but it was strange to us. Maybe we also started to feel the results of all the changes we had gone through in the last few years. However, we tried to make the best of our situation. We were glad to be together and glad that neither Petr nor I had to work at jobs that took us away from home. Besides our work, we had time for our children. We read together, played games, sang songs, told stories. It all filled up our evenings. Later, Tom's teacher gave us a black and white television, but its receiver was not good, so we did not use it often.

We also made some new friends, who put more color in our lives. We met an older couple, where the man was originally from Slovakia. He mentioned that nobody around here spoke our language until our arrival. He and his wife welcomed us and often invited us to their house. We even had a Christmas dinner together. The lady was very devoted to volunteer work. I remember how she baked Christmas cakes and cookies, which she delivered to old people who were unable to bake for themselves. Years later, her husband wrote to us that his wife still baked before Christmas as if an army lay close and would need provisions. Our new friend sometimes took us fishing, a popular leisure activity in Ignace. In the summer, we used his boat, in the winter we went ice-fishing.

We also had our own ideas of how to use frozen lakes. On Boxing Day we drove to Dryden and bought cross-country skiis for the whole family. Weather permitted and we went skiing. Usually, we followed a snowmobile trail. It was bumpy to ski this way, but much easier than to make our own track. With lakes and swamps frozen over, we could get to locations which were inaccessible to us in summer. However, many times we had to be satisfied with a short outing, usually on the power line close to our house. Due to cold weather, we were unable to stay outside longer.

Our children soon found new friends and Kate also started babysitting. She was very proud to make her own money. At the beginning of the school year, both children were placed in a special program for English. Kate attended for only two months and easily caught up with her classmates. On the other hand, Tom visited the special education teacher for the whole year. His teacher prized him and Tom liked it more than his regular class. I did not find out until the next year that Tom, in this way, actually missed some other subjects. Both children later confessed that they had problems with some schoolmates. Unlike their first school, where everybody had tried to help them, in Ignace the children called Kate and Tom immigrants, laughed at them and mocked their accent. I knew from Tom's teacher that there were many problems in the school with discipline, smoking and drugs. Many students came from mining families and often moved from one location to another. Unfortunately, even teachers often changed, to the detriment of the school's reputation.

In front of the cottage with
Andrysek family.

Our first Christmas in
Canada.

With our sponsors before moving to north-western Ontario.

The sawmill camp near Ignace.

Canoing by Ignace.

Hiking in north-western Ontario — lakes everywhere.

14
Moving to Alberta

"Imagination was given to man to compensate him for what he isn't. A sense of humor was provided to console him for what he is." —
Horace Walpole

The sawmill operation began to show some problems before Christmas and they intensified in the New Year. The sawmill did not bring in the expected profit. Mr. Kanes started to pay out only advances, the rest of the wages he kept back until the turn-over would improve. However, productivity fell rather than improving. By spring, the sawmill had lost two groups of contractors who worked in the forest under Petr's supervision. Only one contractor stayed, and this meant Petr did not have enough work. His only option was to start working in the sawmill itself. When I finished my English classes, I returned to work in the kitchen, but my wages were also cut. I had to find another job to make more money and to boost our dwindling budget. Finally, I found a housekeeping position in the local hotel. The wage was only four dollars per hour, but we had regular hours and we also did the hotel's laundry. So in six hours, I made the same money as working for the whole day in the kitchen. On top of this, the hotel was located very close to our place, so I did not need to arrange transportation. I was not afraid of any work, but I felt sorry that I could not work in my forestry profession, for which I had training and education. A forestry position would bring not only more money, but also more joy for me. So far, I had no opportunity for fulfilling work. The town was small, with restricted work opportunities.

When the sawmill conditions became worse, I would sometimes be overtaken by sullen thoughts. In order to relieve stress, I developed what I called "internal pictures." I focussed on moments of my life, some filled with joy but even some anxious times. I recalled my sister, my brothers, my classmates, and my friends. In my imagination, I visualized each detail, whether of people's faces or of landscapes. In my mind, I worked through the problems which had occurred in our lives and which were presently behind us. I most enjoyed remembering the moments of fun, happiness and contentment. In this way, I somehow settled accounts with my life or maybe I just gathered strength from previous experiences. In the end, it was not long before change again came into our lives.

First, we met the wife of a local doctor. He was Chinese and I did not dream that his wife could be a Czech. We saw him when Tom cut his finger while making a bird-feeder. Tom got seven stitches and the doctor learned we were from Czechoslovakia. He used his two sentences, his total knowledge of the Czech language, surely to my astonishment. I was even more surprised when, one evening, his wife came to visit us together with her mother from Calgary. We talked the whole evening. How beautiful the stories about the mountains sounded to us!

Meanwhile, the sawmill operation slowed down considerably, so Petr also had to look for another job. At this time our new friend from Calgary asked Petr to help her by driving her daughter's car back there. Petr agreed with pleasure. He stayed in Calgary for couple of days and visited Banff and the surrounding area. He watched herds of wapiti around the town of Banff and he saw mountains — and that was the end of our stay in Ignace. The Bow Valley was exactly the place we had dreamed of reaching, the end to our wandering. Petr came home ready to pack our belongings and move right away. Meanwhile, I also had made some contacts. One afternoon the hotel owner started a conversation with me. He was originally from Holland and he remembered his own start in Canada. He asked me about our land of origin and how we got to Ignace. When I mentioned my forestry education and how we didn't have much luck with our first jobs in Canada, he paid close attention. Finally, he said that many people from the Ministry of Natural Resources were his customers, so he could ask about a job for me. Of course, we had applied there before, so I did not hope for any results. Suddenly, just two days later, Petr and I were both called for interviews. Within a week we would both start new jobs.

It was just unbelievable! I felt like I was living in a fairy tale. I will always remember the hotel owner as somebody who was willing to step in and help without the need for much talk. His mention of us to ministry personnel came at just the right time. The Ministry of Natural Resources had just opened hiring for the summer positions, but we had not heard yet about seasonal jobs. Ignace, being a small town, did not have many people qualified for the positions, so we fitted right in. I got a half-time position with Fish and Wildlife. To my alarm, I would have to work with a computer. I had never had a chance to do so before this. Back in Czechoslovakia, we always sent our data to computer stations, so we saw the results but never the process. Suddenly, I had to not only input the data but also create new programs, which would summarize the information from department files. During the first days, the computers "beeped" often when I made errors and sometimes my laboriously-entered data was erased. But after a while, everything settled down and I guess I did the work to the satisfaction of my boss. Petr got a job with Forestry out in the field. He worked in a forestry orchard, where young trees were grafted with branches from selected old trees and forced to produce cones quickly. The seed was then used for reforestation of clearcuts and burned areas. It was a very interesting job. However, as he was working outside, the job came with a risk of mosquito and black fly bites. Petr did not like to use any spray but after a while he was forced to change his mind. Soon, he was the biggest user of insect repellent in our family.

We still had to somehow get our money from the sawmill owner. By the time Petr quit, the amount owing was already five thousand. However, we still felt sorry for the owners. The sawmill had nearly stopped producing, more workers left and only a couple of Finns remained. When we expressed our feelings in front of some friends who knew the situation, they just laughed at us. The sawmill really did not work properly because the machinery was old, and had been bought used, making it even less efficient. Mr. Kanes, in the meantime, started to put together another business. At the same time that he was keeping back most of our wages and paying us only a minimum amount to survive, he was buying a huge hunting business with airplanes and lodges, which was apparently worth millions. At first, we did not want to believe it. How could somebody, who was so friendly to us, who knew our situation, behave in this way? Unfortunately, it was true. Finally, on the advice of friends, we applied for help to the local representative of the Ministry of Labour. Of course, we were not the only people to ask for their help in Mr. Kanes's case. We did not know how the process worked but our application was successful: we received two thousand dollars before we left Ignace, the remaining three thousand came in the fall.

Meanwhile, the last signs of the hard winter disappeared. The snow melted, the ice on the lakes broke and melted away. Cir, who liked swimming, did not wait until all the ice disappeared and joyfully jumped into frigid lakes and creeks. We followed his example much later. Unfortunately, we found spring to be the worst time for outdoor walks. The ground was still frozen so the melted snow and ice flooded the trails at lower elevations. If we wanted to make even a short trip, we had to follow only the highest ground. Once we discovered a cliff which towered over the rolling country. Happily we climbed it and sat on the top, overlooking the close lakes and valleys around us. Suddenly, five large birds with enormous wingspans approached the cliff, flying over the tops of the jack pines. I had never seen anything similar. At home, I identified them as turkey vultures. We learned later, the cliff was their nesting place. Otherwise, in our free time, we again made many canoe trips — this time using our own canoe, bought from a man who had canoed in it though most of northern Ontario. It was an aluminium canoe with a wide bottom, excellent even in shallow rivers and creeks. We called it "Big Bertha." She was a little slow for lakes, but always safe. Once we used her for fishing, right after the ice broke and the water was high. A creek, which connected two lakes, was suddenly swollen to a rushing river. I appreciated our safe canoe, when we paddled through the flooded bush trying to avoid drifting logs and wood. We did not catch any fish on this occasion, unlike Tom. Tom was on our friend's boat and had help with the catch but, still, he was very proud.

Also, that spring, we nearly lost our dog. Our neighbors had a new puppy and our children, with Cir, used to visit them and play together. One evening we heard cars braking, a crash and the rattling of hubs on the gravel road. When we ran out of the house, the first thing we saw was the neighbors' children with the puppy. They pointed in alarm to Cir, who was in the ditch and trying to stand up. The driver, an older man, felt guilty and explained that Cir had jumped suddenly into the road — probably when he saw the pup. The driver was not able to stop quickly enough. I knew it was not the driver's fault so I tried hard to calm him. In the meantime, I watched with anxiety as Cir, who had fallen again, showed distress as his legs started to twist as if in cramps and blood could be seen at his mouth. I thought he must have internal injuries and these must be his last movements. There was no veterinarian in town, nor could we afford to pay if there had been one. With the help of our crying children, I moved Cir to our yard (Petr was not home). I was sure I could not help him, so I sadly began to wash the blood and dust from his head. To our surprise, it worked a miracle. The cramping stopped and Cir opened his eyes. We washed him all over. Cir staggered and tried to take a couple of steps. It was difficult, but with our help he made it to the house. When I carefully checked him, I found he had been hit on his head. Three of his teeth were broken. We found a piece of his fang, a couple of weeks later, in his cheek. Fortunately the blood in his mouth came from the broken teeth, not from an internal injury. The cramps were probably due to shock. Cir did not move much for three days and we had to help him go out and come in. He ate nothing and had only a bit to drink. For nearly two months he could not see out of one eye. How happy we were, when at last he could see again! To our joy, he recovered completely.

Soon after the ice broke, spring jumped directly into summer. Petr, in his thoughts, was already in the mountains. It did not matter to him that presently we both had jobs. Impatiently, we waited for the end of school. My work with Fish and Wildlife was scheduled for two months, so I finished at the start of July. Petr's work, however, was projected to last through summer and his workmate mentioned that there was a good chance it would continue afterwards. He himself had been hired just for a season, but he had been working ever since, and was already in his fourth season. However, Petr had decided to move and he did not even consider this possibility. The pull of the mountains was much stronger than anything else. Petr was also putting his faith in promises of work, which he had gotten on his trip to Banff.

So, at the start of July, we moved again. We said good-bye to our friends, who mostly approved of our moving. We had to buy a small trailer to move all the things with which we did not want to part: beds and the freezer. Even our camper was more heavily loaded with new possessions; however, we still had room to cook and sleep comfortably. So, with the camper and trailer, we set out again on the road west, modern nomads in this large and beautiful country. I remember a statistic, that about eight million people were always on the move world wide. We could not imagine so many people, but we definitely met many loaded cars and trucks running in both directions. I wondered how many plans, dreams and hopes, probably resembling our own, we passed on the road in those days.

For the first part of our trip to Manitoba's boundary, we drove through a forested area with many lakes, like that around Ignace. Then came the prairies. In Manitoba, we admired the tidy farms with large pretty houses, which testified to the well-being of their owners. In Saskatchewan, the prairie rolled more and huge ranches took the place of grain farms. Often, we saw pronghorn antelope grazing among the cattle. It was something new for us. In some places we were surprised with a view of salt lakes or the dry, white depressions where the remaining sediment was salt. Otherwise, we thought, both provinces had the same landscape character: wide open grassland country under bright sunlight from early morning to evening. Trees grew only around farmhouses or in ravines and in depressions near the creeks. The huge grain silos located by railroad stations were the most prominent landmarks.

This trip was not just for pleasure; we had a fixed target — the mountains. We did not want only to reach them, we wanted to stay there. Of course, we enjoyed seeing a new part of Canada. The prairies attracted us with their open, expansive landscape and the sun all day long over our heads. However, we could not imagine living there. We crossed two time zones, and gained two hours. At each sign announcing entrance to another province, we took pictures. We photographed the sign "Hwy 1 West." Finally, the most welcome sign said "ALBERTA." The landscape did not differ from that of the previous two provinces but the weather changed for the worse, with a strong wind. We experienced a terrific view of whirling dark clouds, full of fine top-soil particles. The clouds moved swiftly, veiling the entire landscape and resembling smoke. Wind vigorously shook our trailer and camper. We were impatient to reach Calgary, but unfortunately, we were not able to see the long awaited mountains because of the clouds. The next day, the wind calmed down and Alberta showed us its clear, blue sky. The attractions of Calgary, the prairie city as we called it, could not fill us with as much enthusiasm as the mountains. Driving from Calgary to the west, on the very next day, we enjoyed the breathtaking panorama of the Rocky Mountains. We were lured to do more sightseeing, like the tourists, and enjoyed the trip as much as any of them, but our first goal was to find jobs and a place to live, so we could stay.

15
Canmore

"The ever-changing moods and lighting on the mountains is a constant delight in my daily life." — Bob Smith

The trip from Calgary to Canmore takes a little more than one hour. The distance is just over 100 kilometres and the Trans Canada Highway has no settlements or towns except for the turn-off to Morley, on the Stoney reserve. The highway has one interesting feature: it jumps directly from prairie to mountain terrain. We found later that the foothills are, in other places, many kilometres wide, gently rolling, and covered with forest. Only in the Bow River Valley, do the mountains directly meet the prairie. We were astonished by the fast change and gained even more respect for the Rocky Mountains. We had read about them and had our own imaginary pictures of them. Now suddenly, they were in front of us: high, rugged, unapproachable — they did not look friendly at all. The steep rocky walls were either completely bare or just partly covered by alpine forest. A person felt like a speck compared to the size of the Rockies. Certainly, the Rocky Mountains are not the Alps, where the slopes are covered by meadows where cattle graze. The Rockies are wild, not tamed by ranching. Only in the foothills do ranchers lease land for summer grazing.

My first impression was modified later when we hiked through the mountains and saw beautiful wild meadows and blue or green lakes. Then my feeling that the Rockies were unapproachable disappeared and evolved into a sense of intimate familiarity.

Before Canmore, on the old highway (today known as Highway 1A) and across the river from Highway 1 (the Trans Canada) is the small town of Exshaw and even more to the east, several houses stand as reminders of the former railroad station. A cement plant is located there today and a magnesium plant operates near Exshaw. Both plants make use of the natural lime deposits as they cut away a part of the mountain slope, leaving a visible scar. It is not a beautiful view, on the access to the mountains, but it is the only industry in the area. We remembered the cement plants back in Czechoslovakia and were pleasantly surprised at the relative lack of dust around the plants in the Bow Valley, which is, in fact, very narrow. The river fills most of the room, especially on first leaving the prairies. The water is wild, not tamed by dams and dikes, so the river's channel wriggles, changes and, from time to time, overflows. The highest water occurs at the end of spring and start of summer, when the snow melts in the mountains. In fall and winter the water is lower. Both Highway 1 and 1A run along the sides of the river and railroad tracks wind between them. The town of Canmore was built up in a place where the valley opens up a little and it is connected today to another, higher valley by a steep road. The town was established near the end of the last century as a mining town, which supplied a newly built railroad with coal. Who knows if the founders also recognized the beauty of the location. The mines had closed in 1979, more than six years before we came. The coal is still there, but the railroad does not need it any more. When we arrived, Canmore's population was about four thousand people and most work was connected with recreation and service industries, either local or in neighboring Banff National Park or Kananaskis Country. The gates to Banff National Park are just west of Canmore, the town of Banff, itself, twenty kilometres further. Kananaskis Country, established for recreation, is located south of Canmore. It was here, that Petr had been promised a job.

First, we tried to confirm work for me. Through another Czech family living in Canmore, Petr got an assurance that I could work at the Banff Centre, in housekeeping. So I would be cleaning again, but this time as a full-time job, not just for a couple of hours a day. Of course, for this job it did not matter that I was overqualified, the usual response when I applied for employment. The Banff Centre for the Arts is located above the town of Banff, on the slopes of Tunnel Mountain. I did not think anybody could find a better place for a school. The sun shines there the whole day, the town is spread out below, everything is bordered by mountains.We found that I could start right away, so we agreed I would begin work two days later. In these two days, we hoped to find a place to live. Our new friend from Canmore, Elizabeth, offered me temporary accommodation in the Banff Centre compound. It was in a dormitory, which was available in summer to seasonal workers. It would not be luxurious, but I could stay there until we found a place for the whole family.

We did not want to live in Banff. The town was too busy with tourism. So we returned to Canmore, which seemed quieter to us and somehow more likeable. We walked down the main street, which in those days still had many empty lots. First we bought ice cream and then looked to see what local real estate agents offered. Rents were much higher here than in Ignace. We would pay at least twice as much for the same size of apartment, and we would be lucky to find a place to rent. In most cases, there were conditions: "No pets" or "No kids." The other option was to buy something. Again, the prices were much higher, even for the cheapest houses.We saw several of these and they all needed a lot of repair. We saw old houses with crooked porches, twisted roofs, and large windows, none of which would open. On top of this, they were not big enough for us. We needed three bedrooms, which were found only in bigger houses. For such a house we would pay a larger mortgage, provided we could get one, still not knowing how it would go with our jobs. Our worries were confirmed when Petr contacted the person who had promised him a job. The budget had been cut and Petr could not start as planned. As we did not have any experience with Unemployment Insurance, we did not know that Petr should have applied right away, in Calgary.

Disappointed, we returned to Calgary and wondered what to do next. With only one confirmed job, paying a wage that was none too high, we had to abandon the idea of buying a house. Linda, our friend from Calgary, who had offered to let us live in her place until we found some accommodation, remembered another possibility. "What about the trailer park?" — the prices for a trailer were much lower, and they usually had two or three bedrooms, even if they were small. So we drove to Canmore again the next day and looked through the trailer park. It was a much nicer place than the one we remembered from Ignace. This one was located on a "peninsula" between two creeks. The prices varied, but it was possible to buy a trailer for $12,000 to $15,000. We had nearly decided to buy one for this price, when we found another for just $6000. The owners had been trying to sell it for more than a year, so they had reduced the price. This trailer was no worse nor any older than the others we had seen. It had only two bedrooms, but a spare room was being used as a laundry room. It would be easy to convert to an additional bedroom. For this price we would not need a loan, as we could pay cash. We quickly agreed to buy it. When we were signing the sales agreement, both parties confessed that they had worried that the other party would change their minds. Petr and I did not believe the low price. The owners did not trust we could pay cash.

A couple of years later, when the price of houses went up, we partly regretted our decision to buy a trailer. However, given our situation in those days, I guess it was the best solution. We would definitely have had a problem if we had been asking for a bank loan. After all, we still did not have a credit card, Petr did not have a job, and our only possession was a twelve-year-old Dodge truck.

The trailer's owners reserved two weeks for moving out. Meanwhile, I started my job in Banff and had to live in the dormitory. The others living there were mostly students from all over Canada. With some of them, I had some longer talks and was surprised how their lifestyle differed from my own student years. They worked not just to support themselves in the next school year, but in many cases, they interrupted their studies to travel. This would have been impossible in my original country. Otherwise, I tried to use my free time for walking and short trips around Banff. The summer was beautiful: hot weather, nearly cloudless blue Alberta skies. Nights in the mountains were cooler, which was pleasant. Petr and children, who still lived in Calgary, complained how hot the city was, even at night. However, they experienced, first hand, the Greatest Outdoor Show of the real western rodeos: the Calgary Stampede. The whole city lived in a festive atmosphere: shops, malls, offices and banks had rodeo decorations. The clerks and salespeople were dressed in western style — if nothing else, they wore a cowboy hat and a scarf around the neck. Petr went with Kate and Tom to see some Stampede attractions and they enthusiastically told me about it afterwards. They went to a free breakfast where a band played country music and some people even danced. On the free day for kids, they went to the Stampede grounds, so excited they did not know where to go first, to the Indian village, to agriculture exhibits, to art exhibitions or just to watch all the action, listen to bands and take rides on carousels. They watched the rodeo and chuckwagon races on television, however, as those tickets were too much for our budget.

One problem appeared with my work — transportation to Banff and back. Our old truck was already showing its age and operating it was expensive. We began to think of buying a small car. A friend of Linda's offered us a used Honda, which needed some fixing. Petr started to work on the body right away, in Calgary, while the friend worked on the engine. Unfortunately, when I started to use the car, another problem with the engine developed. Fixing this would be more expensive than the car itself. For a while, I used an invitation of my co-workers, who lived in Canmore, to ride with them. After we finally got our money from Ignace, we decided to buy a new car. Of course, we picked the cheapest one for sale in Canmore, but I hoped it would be reliable. And it was! I had been losing trust in buying used cars, mostly because we were often not able to fix them ourselves. The car loan for two years went smoothly, so we became owners of a car and a trailer, even if it was just an old one. Most importantly, we had a credit rating.

We were happy when we could move into our trailer. I had two days off, which I planned to use for organizing our household. However, the weather was so beautiful, it was tempting to go out. It did not take much time to move, so on the second day we decided to climb one of the surrounding mountains, Grotto Mountain, hoping to view Canmore from the top. We did not know if there was a trail, so we just decided, after studying it from our viewpoint, where to start and how to move up. We did not even take a pack or any water, just some fruit. Going by our experience in the Alps, we had always run into some water. Unfortunately, this was not true in Canmore. The only water was in Cougar Creek, where we started our ascent. How we were thinking about water for the whole climb up, on the south side of the mountain, all day in the full sun! However, the view from the top was incredible, quite worth our effort. Other peaks and valleys appeared in front of us inviting us to explore them.

The hot summer continued until August. The grass around the trailer was burned, so we did not need to take up that popular summer activity: to mow our lawn, water it, fertilize and mow again. Our children and Petr made full use of the beautiful summer. They took some trips and explored our surroundings and in my time off, they showed me the most attractive places. They only missed out on outdoor swimming, as the river and lakes were unbearably cold. Later, a friend from Calgary remembered how he had tried to swim in the Spray Lakes above Canmore. He said it was such a hot day the blue lake just lured them in. He and his friend did not think twice and jumped into the lake — only to jump out even faster! Finally, close to Banff, we found Johnson Lake, which was enlarged by construction of a dam, had shallow water at one end, and served well for outdoor swimming. However, its water was still very "refreshing." Even better was a former quarry located directly above Canmore. There was no tributary to the lake formed in the former quarry, so the surface water had a chance to warm up. The access to the water was through some coal deposits. A couple of years later, the town groomed the area, covered the coal with sand and turned the whole quarry into a recreation area. Since then, we evaluate how warm each summer is according to a count of our swims in Quarry Lake.

Quarry Lake area was actually the first place where I applied my conservation attempts in Canada. Based on my sad knowledge of natural degradation from Europe, I wanted to help protect nature here in Canada. Unfortunately, I found that a lot of conservation organizations just ask for donations. On top of this, there was not too much co-ordination between them. The local naturalists' organization gave me a much better feeling of participation. They organized lectures, slide-shows, and outings which I really enjoyed. They informed about local issues, as well as about Alberta, British Columbia, and wider issues. They also suggested where our voices should be heard and to whom to write. It was encouraging to find that a loud public protest could alter political decisions. On the other hand, as "money and power talk," in some cases, the protests did not help. I have, at home, several thank-you letters from politicians for my efforts to support the plans for new natural reserves and protected areas. However, I received more satisfaction from the feeling that some parts of this beautiful country would remain in their natural state.

The issue of Quarry Lake arose when a developer from Calgary proposed to build an RV park around the lake. I joined with other protesters who viewed the area as well-suited for local recreation, and hoped for upgrading but not development. We collected signatures and finally won the "first round" for Quarry Lake. The area was really improved, but a few years later, we had to fight another "developer."

Of all possible activities near Canmore, we adults prefered hiking. As I worked during the day, we went out in the evenings. The days seemed to be longer than in Europe and we tried to use all our free time to become familiar with our new environment. A couple of weeks after we moved to Canmore, Elizabeth introduced us to friends from northern British Columbia. They travelled nearly every year to the Rocky Mountains and always spent a part of their holidays hiking. Their son was same age as Tom and they were instantly buddies. Our new friends offered to take Tom with them for a four-day trip, as the boys would have more fun together. In those days we did not have any equipment for backcountry camping, only one down sleeping bag, still from Czechoslovakia, but Tom did not need anything more. Feeling a little envy, we told Tom and his friend "Good-bye." Afterwards it hit me that we also could go, at least for one night. It was exactly what we wanted — to make a backcountry trip, staying overnight. I was aware the warm weather could not last long and who knew when we would have another opportunity. The only problem was the lack of equipment. Finally, we borrowed a two-person tent and packed cheap sleeping bags, which we also borrowed. We did not have any camping stove or outdoor utensils, so we hoped to cook over a fire.

The hike was beautiful. After some climbing, we went through an alpine meadow, full of wildflowers. Just the colorful view alone filled me with excitement. The alpine meadows were the highlight of our hikes in the Alps and I was happy to see them here, in the Rockies. They were more wild but equally beautiful. Not far from the meadows, we spotted mountain goats. We observed them for a while with binoculars, as it was our first time to see them. Close to the lakes, where our friends were camped, we passed a marmot colony. The young ones and their parents whistled and watched us with curiosity. When we arrived, our friends and Tom were surprised to see us. However, they immediately offered us some trout which they had caught. The fishing was the best they had experienced and they told us that the lakes were boiling with trout. We, of course, had not brought a fishing rod, even though we had a fishing licence for the park. Tom found a solution. He ran around the lakes and collected left-over fishing equipment: lines, hooks, and weights. Using a stick, we made a rod and also tried our luck. However, the trout had apparently lost their appetites as they did not take our bait.

The night was wild — at least for us. The temperature, which was over 27°C during the day, dropped below zero. In the morning, everything was frosty and frozen. We shivered with cold in our thin sleeping bags without thermal mattresses. The two-person tent had to accommodate not only three of us, but also Cir. We were worried about leaving him outside as we had seen a porcupine in the campground. It rested in a tree beside a campground outhouse, which was half missing. Apparently, the porcupine had chewed away the top half. At night, it walked through the campground, loudly sniffing and chewing whatever it found. When we heard it by our tent we were happy that Cir was inside. After the uncomfortable night — cold, sore and sleepy, I made a vow that we would buy proper equipment for backcountry camping. After we had breakfast and warmed up by the morning fire, we again tried our fishermen's luck. This time, we did not believe our eyes! As we did not have any bait, we just killed some horseflies, threw them into the lake and right away the water boiled with fish. When we threw in our line, we had a trout. Kate and Tom tried first, then Petr. I did not have a chance, as we had our limit. How different this was from just sitting and waiting with a rod! And the fish were delicious! Later, we observed more mountain goats and I identified some wild flowers. Over all, it was a great trip, even with the uncomfortable night.

Our next excursion was to Elk Lake, about a one-hour drive through the beautiful Kananaskis Valley. We had a picnic on the shore of the mountain lake with our new friends and, as it was Kate's birthday, she felt it was a real celebration. The drive had looked far to me, but later we became used to driving such distances without even thinking about it. From the parking lot, we made a comical sight as we walked up a steep hill to the lake, lugging the food piled in our outstretched hands. At this time, there was a suspicion about water-borne infection and the resulting sickness, "beaver fever." Our friends carried several bottles of drinking water, and strictly prohibited their children from drinking water from the lake or streams. It surprised us. Of course we would not drink from lakes or creeks, but we prized the purity of small streams and were proud that we could use them to drink from, unlike the situation in our old country, where it was impossible.

Elk Lake and the surrounding area were beautiful. Kate, Tom, and the other children tried their luck fishing, but without success. Petr and I went for a short walk further up the valley. We were tempted to go much further, but the time for such trips came years later. Toward the day's end, the temperature dropped and we had to put on warmer clothing. The hot summer was over.

After a couple of weeks, we began to know our immediate surroundings. It did not matter where we went, Canmore, Banff, Spray or Barrier Lakes, we never tired of mountain views, the changing color of the lakes, or watching wildlife. Banff National Park, especially, gave many opportunities to watch wapiti, deer, sheep and moose. Once, at Vermillion Lakes close to Banff, we saw a moose grazing on water plants across from a herd of elk, while above them, a bald eagle watched from a tree. Unfortunately, some animals lost their natural wariness and grazed in parks or private yards in the Banff townsite. The Banff Centre, which is oriented to the south, was regularly visited by herds of elk. They grazed or rested on lawns, completely unmindful of human presence. It was nearly impossible to keep ornamental trees and shrubs undamaged, even with wire fencing and burlap covers in winter. I often saw how elk debarked or otherwise destroyed trees or lawns. In the fall rut, we had to run from one building to another, as the elk viewed the area as their home and humans as intruders. However, I have to admit, I was pleased to observe them in the course of my otherwise monotonous work.

Slowly, we discovered the other advantages of Banff. Our wish for outdoor swimming was completely satisfied in the hot springs. The Cave and Basin became our favorite and we used it on cooler days. After the pool closed for the season, we began to visit the Banff Centre pool and sauna. An even more pleasant discovery was the theatre at the Banff Centre. Artists and performers from Canada and abroad, engaged in a wide variety of performance art, dance and ballet, as well as drama, comedy or opera and gave concerts ranging from classical to jazz. One could visit art exhibits at the Centre and downtown. The Banff Centre also hosted festivals, among them the Mountain Film Festival in November and the Television Festival in June. I was very happy to find such a variety of cultural experience and was very glad that my children had so many opportunities to be exposed to it.

16
Settled In

"If I were the king of the world I would turn Canada, the whole country , into an international park. An international ecological megagarden. That would be the best possible future for Canada."
— Tomson Highway

We modified the trailer to meet our needs, changing the laundry room to become Kate's "mini" room. Petr made a bed and we put on new wallpaper. The washing machine fitted into our bathroom and we put the dryer on the porch. What we were missing was a workshop and a storage room. We were also thinking about a wood stove, but there was no room for it. Finally, Petr decided to build an addition which could fulfill all our requirements, including the wood stove. In the fall, Petr still did not have a job, despite several applications. A friend convinced him to apply for Unemployment Insurance in November. Of course, it was late and Petr was penalized. More than half a year passed before he got any money. Once more, we paid for our unfamiliarity with bureaucratic systems.

In the fall, Petr went hunting. He was glad that he had met some new friends, who also enjoyed the sport, in Calgary, as going alone would be difficult. He did not know the area, and game, such moose or elk, is too heavy to handle alone. On one hunting trip Petr found an old abandoned shed. He asked the rancher for a permit to dismantle it and then we used the boards for our addition. The best colored boards, which had a reddish-black tone, we used on the inside.

Our children started a new school year, now attending their fifth school since our escape. The school was only five minutes walking distance from the trailer park, so they did not need to ride a school bus. Both Tom and Kate liked the Canmore school and it was only now that they told us about their difficulties in Ignace. About a month later, I was called to the school and Tom's teacher recommended moving Tom back to grade four. This meant repeating a grade, which Tom had finished in Ignace with very good marks. I was a little in shock. However, the teacher was right. She explained to me that Tom had missed some other subjects due to his special English program, and above all, his English vocabulary was still very poor. According to her, children build their vocabulary between grade one and three. Unfortunately for Tom, this was exactly the time when his language of instruction was changed three times. Both the teacher and the principal, who joined the meeting, assured me that it would only benefit Tom and was nothing to be ashamed of. They promised to explain the situation in both classrooms. I could not judge Tom's progress in English myself, but I knew he had a restricted word supply even in Czech. When I agreed, the teacher explained everything to Tom and that evening at home, we discussed it with him again. However, Tom took it as a shameful thing and he did not feel comfortable in his new classroom for two months. Eventually he found new friends and that helped him to fit in. We implemented strict rules at home. Tom had to read to us daily and then explain the context. It was, of course, also a demand on our time, to support his efforts and to work with him each day, but it paid off. I personally believe repeating the grade did not harm Tom at all and helped him manage his school much more easily afterwards, as his grades were usually over eighty percent.

Kate did not have any problems. In fact, she soon became one of the best students. All through junior high school she got awards for being the top student in her classroom. I was most impressed that she managed to win even the English award!

Right after we moved to the trailer park, a distributor for the Calgary Herald convinced our children to deliver newspapers. Kate and Tom split their route, which included the whole trailer park and some adjacent streets. Each day, before they went to school, they each delivered half of the newspapers. At the end of each month, they shared the money, proud to make their own cash, as they did not get any pocket money from us.

In the fall, Tom met a very interesting man. Tom had an ability to easily meet people and talk with them about anything. I doubt that he inherited this ability from us — we did not make new friends so readily, especially as we did not yet feel confident due to our imperfect language. Tom was, at this time, enthusiastic about making Indian artifacts, such as bows and arrows and he had just completed a feather headdress. One day Tom came home very happy, as a friend had introduced him to a man who had lived for several years in the north. According to Tom, this man was capable of making "real" bows and arrows, and he knew a lot about it. After several visits with him, just a few trailers from ours, Tom finally introduced him to us. So we met

Don, probably the most interesting person we had met so far in Canada. Don not only made absorbing conversation, he also listened with attention. We definitely did not say everything properly in English, but he never asked, "What?" He always managed to translate our words, answered right away or asked questions so that he fully understood us. We felt very easy with him and talked freely. It was a real contrast to the usual situation where people would ask us about our lives, how we got to Canada and how we liked it here, but by their second or third question we would find that they did not really listen or perceive what we said. It was different with Don and we really appreciated him for it. The thing we loved most was to listen to his stories.

Don had studied Archeology and spent six seasons in the Arctic doing archeological research. He knew not only a lot about bows and arrows, the areas of their origin and how they were used, but also about other artifacts. He occasionally made replicas for museums and used only authentic tools to produce them. Unless he was travelling, he worked at his own business of designing and building recreational ski trails. Before the winter Olympics in 1988, he designed the cross-country trails at the new Canmore Nordic Centre. He was formerly a top cross-country racer in Canada and related many of his ski experiences with humor. He was also an excellent climber and known in the climbing community for his free technique as well as for his first ascents. In spite of all his knowledge and popularity, Don was very modest and we often had to nearly force him to tell us about himself. Don knew and travelled through the mountains like nobody we had met before. He and some friends had made the first ski traverse though all the mountain parks some years earlier. He was a ready source of information of where to go, what to see there, and what we should not miss. Don could talk about anything and was interested in everything, so his visits became the most enjoyable events in our family. Kate and Tom, who did not have any relatives in Canada, soon adopted Don as their "uncle."

So we settled in, becoming familiar with our surroundings and meeting new friends. Before winter, Petr built the addition. At a garage sale, we bought a small wood stove, which gave us a pleasant and cheap additional source of heat. We were not enthusiastic about living in the trailer park, as we felt a little "squeezed" there; however, we did not see any other solution. In the first few weeks, I heard Czech being spoken in the neighborhood. It surprised me and I went to introduce myself. Our neighbors were a young couple with a small daughter, the only other Czech family in the trailer park. Even though they had different interests, it was nice to have neighbors to stop to chat with in our native language.

I must tell about one more friend, Gretchen, whom I met the same fall. Her son was already friendly with Tom. Gretchen was a French teacher but she offered to help me work on my English.We had no money to spare, but Gretchen's solution was to offer free lessons. It was very enjoyable not only to continue to refine my English with superb guidance, but also to spend time in the pleasant surroundings of Gretchen's home. We discussed all kinds of themes and I believe most of my progress in English was due to conversations with Gretchen.

Gretchen later invited me to take part in the weekly trips, which she and her friends regularly made on Wednesdays. They hiked in summer and did back-country skiing in winter. I happily accepted and took part whenever I had a day off, hiking and skiing with them on many trails and in many places where I did not have a chance to go with my family nor the courage to go by myself. It was not only the sightseeing which made these trips highlights of my days. Above all, it was meeting with new friends, women of a similar age to myself, who always had something in common to talk about. We had a lot of fun and I was always grateful to them for receiving me so nicely. After a time, our numbers increased from the original four to six until we were ten to fifteen, and our trips reminded me of school outings. Some of us were worried about meeting bears, but I doubt a bear could endure to be close to us. When such a "flock" of women started to march and discuss all kinds of events which had happened since we last saw each other, not only bears, but all other wildlife, probably ran away. We even named our group the "Bow Valley Playgirls." Besides the trips, we occasionally had social evenings together which were, again, events to remember.

All in all, our life in Canmore was comfortable. Only our work was not the work we wanted to do. We applied for jobs, answered ads, talked to friends and followed their recommendations, all in vain. One of my first inquiries led to the local forestry office. Their answer was, "Maybe in the spring." Among all the negative answers, I was sure that it did not mean anything. So far, I had to be happy just to have regular work. After a couple of months, I was accepted as a permanent worker with benefits, such as medical care and later dental care. It was an asset, but did not make me happier.

After the summer months, most of the students, with their amusement lifestyle, left and only permanent workers stayed. It was very quiet at the Banff Centre. At the start, I cleaned thoroughly but slowly. Then I desperately rushed to finish my section, sometimes even with help from other staff. As I got faster, the supervisors praised me for my work, as it was done well and on time. This praise was the only pleasure I got from my job. No, in fact, I had one more daily pleasure: the view of the mountains. How they changed according to the weather! They were grey and unapproachable in the rain or veiled in clouds and fog, with the sometimes surprising emergence of their tops above the clouds. However, the most beautiful view was in full sun, when the gorgeous blue sky contrasted with white capped peaks. For the whole first year of driving through the Bow Valley corridor, I did not get tired of admiring the spectacular view. As for Petr, he did not get any work until spring. It was a financial relief, at least, when he finally got UI benefits.

The winter started abruptly. A cold wave arrived on Halloween. Trick-or-treaters were shivering when they came to the door. The temperature dropped below -30° Celsius and it lasted six weeks. After living in Ignace, we did not consider this as something exceptional. Despite this, everybody in Canmore assured us that this was not normal and that a Chinook should come soon. Chinooks are warm winds, coming from the Pacific ocean, over the mountains. They bring snow sometimes, but west of the Rockies and in south-western Alberta, Chinooks become evident as a sudden warm-up. Later we found out for ourselves how the temperature would abruptly jump from lows of -15° to highs of +10° Celsius. After a while, we learned to recognize the typical Chinook clouds which announced the arrival of the warm wind. We also experienced the feeling of tiredness, due to the sudden change of atmospheric pressure. In general, however, Chinooks were a welcome break in winter. Winters in Canmore were usually warmer than in Ignace, even without the Chinooks. Average temperatures were comparable to those in our old country, in the mountains where we lived. In drawing this parallel, there is one great exception. We found more sunny days in Canmore. I remember that in Europe the winter days were grey and cloudy with high humidity. Here the air was much dryer and many days were sunny, with beautiful blue skies bordered by the white mountains. This view could improve even the worst mood.

The long waited Chinook finally came just before Christmas, with such high temperatures that it melted all the snow around Canmore. We did not know that further into the mountains there was still enough snow to ski. On Christmas day, we changed our long-antici-pated ski trip to go hiking. We drove along the foothills to the north, crossed the Red Deer River and came to the beautiful meadows called Ya-ha-tinda. The mountains surrounded the meadows like a wall and made the place a natural overwintering ground for game. Today, the park wardens use the area for their horses as Banff National Park adjoins the meadows on the west. The horses share the Ya-ha-tinda with huge herds of elk. When we arrived, the snow was gone and we had a good hike.

When I remember this Christmas, I could not omit mentioning a surprise invitation. On December 23, the telephone rang and complete strangers invited us to celebrate Christmas with them. It was a young couple, originally from the United States, who usually celebrated the holidays with their friends and children. They told us that their parents could not visit them this year, so they had decided to invite somebody else. Somehow they had found out that we were newcom-ers and invited us. As I have already mentioned, for us the biggest celebration is on Christmas Eve, when we prefer our privacy. We gladly accepted the invitation for the next day, however. When we arrived, their children were already playing with new toys and our children joined them. The supper was excellent and we enjoyed this unexpected social event very much.

After the next snowfall, we started skiing and "discovered" superb groomed cross-country ski trails such as we had never experienced before. Back in Czechoslovakia and in Germany we always broke our own trails, sometimes in deep snow. In Ontario, we were happy to follow snowmobile trails in spite of bumpy skiing. Suddenly, we were skiing on well-groomed trails, which were often renewed. Even when the snow everywhere else was getting icy due to warming and freez-ing conditions, the trails were as if on fresh snow. Our enthusiasm for cross-country skiing increased even more. Most of all, Kate and Tom started to really like it. It was more fun to ski on hilly trails than on the flat lakes of Ontario.

Both Kate and Tom were eager to take advantage of other sports opportunities at school as well as after school. In Canmore, there were definitely more opportunities than in Ignace. Kate liked gymnastics and figure skating and presently she did not know which one to take. She tried both, but with unfortunate results. She found that she was joining the sport too late. Girls of her age were already in the advanced classes and Kate had to take classes with little girls. Kate had grown very fast and was one of the tallest in her classroom, even though most of her classmates eventually outgrew her. In her gymnastics and, later, her figure-skating class, Kate towered over the smaller children and looked like their teacher. It was discouraging, and she searched for another sport, where she could be with girls of her own age.

Tom was keen to play hockey. No wonder, it was a popular spectator sport and played everywhere. Each hamlet and village had at least an outdoor rink and towns had indoor hockey rinks and recreation centres. Of course, Canmore had a nice indoor facility. Unfortunately, we found on registration night that this sport was beyond our financial means. Both our children knew about our financial situation, as we discussed it in front of them, so despite his disappointment, Tom admitted that hockey would not be "his sport" but, at least, he enjoyed the outdoor rink in the trailer park, where he played hockey with other boys according to their own informal rules.

In this fashion, winter came to a close and spring came. However, it was not like any spring which we knew from Europe or Lindsay — a spring with flower beds and fruit trees gradually coming into blossom. Our location in the mountains, with its high elevation, did not give much of a chance for early spring flowers and none at all for fruit trees. They could not withstand the harsh and changeable weather. Most houses did not have any flower beds as their owners cared only about their lawns. So spring just suddenly arrived. Temperatures went up quickly, but later it cooled down. At night, frost came. We had rain, then snow again, and suddenly we jumped into summer. We had probably the best moments of the spring in the higher elevations, where we skiied just in T-shirts, the children even in shorts. Sunglasses were a "must" as the sun was very strong. The forest was already awakened from winter's spell. It smelled fresh from balsam and the open ground, which showed around the base of some trees. Sometimes we sat on the open ground and just watched the deep blue of the sky and the white topped mountains all around.

In this year, the spring break occurred at Easter. Even though we liked spring skiing very much, we looked forward to hiking deep into the mountains. However, there was no chance until late May or June, when the snow melted. So we decided instead to do another "discovery" trip. Back in Ontario, when I wrote my letters of application, I got responses from two Czech foresters in British Columbia. They had read our applications to their employers and one family with four children had stayed in touch with us. Now, we decided to use their invitation and drove to their home town, Prince George.

Another goal of our trip was in northern Alberta. We had an interesting reason to go there. We would pick up two puppies, whose father was our own dog, Cir. In the previous fall, another Czech had introduced himself to us. He had been in Canada barely one year but he knew of us from Czechoslovakia — in particular, he knew that we had a bloodhound with us. As he raised the same breed of dog, before he fled the country he had picked a bitch which would suit our dog. When we met, my question was, as usual, "How did you manage to escape?" In his case, it was not too exciting. He had worked in forestry close the Czech-Austrian border. In front of the boundary line was a strip of land, fenced and inaccessible to the average citizen. Nevertheless, the forestry workers would go behind the fence, as the area was in their jurisdiction, usually with soldiers along, but often they were not guarded. So our friend took his packsack with some necessities and his dog, peacefully walked behind the fence as usual on these occasions, and did not stop until he reached Austria. A year ago, his co-worker had fled in much the same way, but assuming a higher risk and taking advantage of working with horses. As in many European countries, game in Czechoslovakia is fed in winter. So this man had loaded up with hay to fill the feeding stations behind the fence. Under the hay, he had hidden his own family and, in addition, the entire family of another friend. He drove through the guarded gate, where they let him go without any suspicion, as it was his daily route. This time, he drove directly to the nearest Austrian village, where they all first applied for status as landed immigrants, and second, he asked if they could return the horses to Czechoslovakia. Both families managed to get to Canada and settled on farms in northern Alberta. When our new friend arrived in Canada, he moved close to them. In the fall, he visited us at the "right time" with his bitch, and the result was five cute puppies.

Prince George is the largest city in northern British Columbia. Like Ignace, it is situated on nearly flat or at most, gently rolling, forested country. The forest industry is concentrated there, with sawmills, pulp mills and manufacturers of wood products. The forest regulations in British Columbia were different from those in Alberta, and clear cuts encompassed huge areas, which "welcomed" us long before we arrived at the city. Thanks to our friend, we later had a closer look at the reforestation of clear cuts. The new growth of trees was most remarkable, and entire areas of clear-cut were green. This closer look moderated our first shock and reminded us of north-western Ontario, where we saw huge areas of burned forest, which vigorously grew again after a while.

We liked these new friends very much. We adults had good chats and the children had a lot of fun together. We have kept in touch ever since. While around Prince George the weather was cloudy, on our return, Alberta again welcomed us with sun and blue sky. It was frosty overnight, but the days were beautiful.

We met our other friend in Beaverlodge and he showed us the puppies. They were now two months old and followed at a run beside their proud mother. It would be hard to resist playing with them! Kate and Tom were happy that we were taking two of them with us, and they would be ours, at least for a while. When we handed them over, a couple of days later, to the new owners, our children regretted that we could not take one home. However, it was impossible, as in the trailer park, it was prohibited to keep any pets. Of course, we were not the only ones with a dog and even more owners had cats. Nevertheless, we were glad that our dog, Cir, was very calm and did not bark, so he did not draw any attention and we did not have any problems.

As the days became longer, the sun climbed higher above the mountain tops. In the winter months, the low sun was soon hidden behind the surrounding mountains. In the course of my work, I would run, during my coffee breaks, up to the top of the building just to watch the mountains. Back in Czechoslovakia, I had worked mostly in the field and I could not get used to working indoors. The mountain scenery was so tempting that I comforted myself with the thought that the views, which visitors pay dearly for, came free with my work.

Our job search continued and Petr and I revisited the employers where we had been promised a chance of an opening in spring. How surprised and happy we were to find that the promises were real! We did not yet understand the system of seasonal positions, even though we had some experience of it in Ignace. Back in our old country, only students worked in summer positions and adults had, predominantly, permanent positions. First, Petr came home with good news. He was hired for trail maintenance in Peter Lougheed Provincial Park. It was outdoor work, which Petr preferred. The park location meant about one hour of driving each way, but Petr could use the employer's vehicle for transportation. Petr liked not only the work, but the whole park. Often he told us about trails and different places in the park and we regretted that we did not have enough time to hike them all together. Petr, apparently, worked out well, as within a month he was promoted to supervising a summer-student crew. Already with higher hopes as a result of Petr's success, I went to the Forestry office. The district officer welcomed me, made a joke that he already waited for me and confirmed that they had gotten funding for a summer position. The work was in forest protection, checking on tree diseases. The first was a kind of cancer, which affected aspen and poplar. After infection, trees usually died and branches would break easily, causing a serious problem in day-use areas and campgrounds. The second problem was with bark beetles on pines. In previous years, Alberta had recorded outbreaks of mountain pine beetles and Forestry was doing everything to keep the attacks under control. So my job was mostly field work as well. I was so happy! I forced myself to keep calm and tried not to show too much joy. However, I guess it was obvious. As I was leaving the office I had the feeling that I was flying! The employment officer made arrangements for my interview and for a meeting with my co-worker.

At the Banff Centre, I announced that I would be leaving my job. Elizabeth understood, as we had talked many times, about my plans and that I had taken my present job as a temporary one. However, some of my co-workers were surprised that I could leave a permanent position for a seasonal one and lose my benefits as well. I could understand their worries, but my philosophy was different. I could not be content in any work just for its security. No benefits could replace the ability to enjoy each day, doing work that I liked, even just for a summer. I had no doubt that I liked my occupation — forester. Even later, when, desperate for any job, I thought to take re-training, I could not find anything else I liked.

The interview went without a problem. The only new thing I would have to learn was a different style of map reading. The mountain pine beetle checking was done in standard ways. One of them was by air survey from a helicopter. As the trees infested in the previous season started to die and changed color to reddish-yellow, they were easily recognized from the air. I had never flown in a helicopter, so I anticipated my first flight with both enthusiasm and worry. It was a great opportunity to see the mountains from the air, especially those places which would take too long to reach on foot or which were otherwise inaccessible. On the other hand, I was worried what my stomach would do. As a child, my stomach was "ticklish" and I had problems with nausea, even in cars. Fortunately, I did not need to be afraid; I felt great and, even later, I was never sick. However, I found out through the next few years, that not every pilot can provide a smooth flight. On my first aerial survey we had an older, experienced pilot, who did not want me to see the rough side of flying. He promised to fly "as if in feathers" — and he kept his word! We flew not only over the older pine stands in our district, but we crossed the continental divide and checked along the boundary into British Columbia. It was actually very close and it was clear that the beetle came to Alberta from the west, in line with prevailing air currents. We found big patches of red trees and noticed how, lower in the valleys, the forestry companies had started to log the infested forest. Throughout the summer we set chemical baits in the pine stands. The chemical stimulated the hormones of both sexes of the beetle and lured them to the baited tree, which was easy to check and eventually exterminate along with the infesting beetles. We also checked the pine stands by walking along previously marked traverse lines.

The second part of our work, checking cancer on aspen trees, was more complicated. It took a little while for our superiors from Calgary to decide to on a way to do the survey. Finally, priority was given to heavily used areas such as campgrounds, day-use areas and trail heads in Kananaskis Country. We also monitored a couple of random plots in the aspen forest for comparison. As a result, I had a great opportunity to travel throughout the whole of Kananaskis Country and to see its recreation areas. I soon had another opportunity to see and hike in a new area, but the purpose of this hike was a sad one. In the middle of the season, a small Cesna airplane was lost one stormy afternoon. On board, besides the pilot, was a researcher studying sheep movements around Mt. Allan and Nakiska. When they did not return to Calgary on time, three of their friends and a pilot took another plane to look for them. They did not return either! Neither plane could be found for several days, so all the government employees from Forestry, Parks, and Fish and Wildlife departments joined the search together with the army. Unfortunately, another disaster happened, the third in a row. An army search plane, carrying crew and volunteers, was caught in the tree tops during take-off and crashed. All eight people on board were killed. Fourteen people altogether had perished. Petr and I took part in some searches. One of the ground searches finally found the remains of the second plane. During the storm, the plane had struck the east peak of Mt. Lougheed and parts were scattered all around. The first plane was found many days later, discovered by the same helicopter pilot who took me on my first flight. This plane had hit a rock wall and literally fallen between the wall and the trees, which grew in front of it. Only one tree was damaged and there was a dark spot on the wall from the resulting fire. The place of impact, where probably both the researcher and the pilot died instantly, was nearly imperceptible. Incidentally, during the day of the first disaster, I and my co-worker were surveying nearby. We hurried to finish as we heard the approaching storm. One of the thunder claps sounded very strange and when we put together the time with the investigators, we found we were probably the only "witnesses," having unknowingly heard the sound of the disaster.

Otherwise, the work brought us more pleasureable moments. I was happy to work in the field, watching the mountains and sometimes wildlife, including my first sight of a black bear. The summer was not as hot as the previous year. Often it rained and some days were very cold. We sometimes got chilled before we finished our daily tasks. My co-worker, a young woman, sometimes objected when I decided to finish work in a particular location in spite of the weather, so we would not need to return the next day. Her position was that seasonal work should not be taken so seriously. For me, it did not matter if I was permanent or seasonal. More important was the question — did I like the work? I knew from experience that each job has its pluses and minuses, its privileges and disadvantages. If there was at least fifty percent pleasure in the work, the negatives could be managed more easily. A rainy day was only a small disadvantage for me. In addition to discussing our views on employment, we had many other discussions during the season, mostly pleasant ones, which again helped my English.

Kate and Tom finished their first school year in Canmore. Both got very good report cards. Kate was a top student in her grade and she got an award for high academic achievement. Tom was rewarded for his stay in grade four. They learned about dinosaurs and Tom loved it! Besides other projects, their class made a huge model of a dinosaur, which was later used in the Canada Day parade on July first. In the parade, Tom, dressed in Native costume, which he had made himself, proudly helped to tow the model. The study of dinosaurs was supported by a school trip to Drumheller, where in the Badlands around the Red Deer River, many remains of the prehistoric lizards had been discovered. Whole and partial skeletons of dinosaurs had been taken ever since from Alberta to museums around the world. Only recently, in 1985, a modern museum was built in Drumheller and visitor use has increased greatly. Most of the children, not to mention Tom, were very excited about the trip. He was so impressed with the museum that he insisted that our whole family go to visit it during our next days off.

With the approach of the summer holidays, we had a problem making arrangements for what our children would do. Officially, they were old enough to be home alone. In fact, they were themselves babysitting younger children. However, they needed some activity, which they would enjoy and which would occupy part of their time. We definitely did not want them to wander aimlessly through the town and to be bored. Kate was always interested in veterinary work. We suggested to her to sign up as a helper at the local veterinary clinic. It would be volunteer work, just for interest. The clinic accepted her, and Kate tried all kinds of work there. To our surprise, at the end of the holiday, she changed her mind and did not want to be a veterinarian any more. Tom loved horses, so he asked around town, discovered who raised them, and finally made an agreement with one owner to help him with feeding and care. Tirelessly, every morning and evening he biked to the stables below the Alpine Club of Canada to help with the chores. I do not know how much help he was but it definitely took a lot of his time. Both Kate and Tom continued to deliver newspapers and had their chores at home, as well as reading in English. I also tried, over the summer holidays, to work with them on Czech spelling and reading. Kate still remembered some things but Tom was hopeless. Sometimes I did not know whether to laugh or weep, as Czech spelling is very complicated and Tom usually picked the wrong letter. When we adults had time, we all continued our exploratory trips. We also pulled out our canoe, at least for use on the closest lakes.

Already, in the winter, we had made more friends. From friends in Toronto, we got the address of a Czech man who escaped from Czechoslovakia after the communist putsch in 1948, so he had been in Canada over forty years. Dennis worked on a long-term forest research project and lived with his family in a nice old log house in the Kananaskis Valley. He could not help us with jobs, but in the summer he invited our children to a summer camp, run by a Czech organization in Calgary, where Dennis had tirelessly worked for years. The location of the camp was in Peter Lougheed Park, where Petr worked. The children lived in tents and teepees and they used a closed shelter for cooking and indoor activities. The organization was not exactly as we adults would have wished, but Kate and Tom liked it. They had the company of other children and a lot of fun.

Petr met another friend, Jim, in his work. Jim was interested in hunting and guns, so they understood each other quickly. Jim initiated us into his hobby, black powder shooting. The people interested in this hobby held regular "Rendez-vous" (meetings) where they competed in black powder shooting and other activities such as knife and tomahawk throwing or bow shooting. The competitors and sometimes their whole families dressed as frontierspeople. Those who were skilled enough made their own costumes and sold or exchanged them for other goods on "Rendez-vous." We saw whole families who specialized in making equipment or clothing: shirts, cups, belts, tomahawks. Everybody looked forward to the next competition to trade or buy goods. The "Rendez-vous" were not organized only within the province, but throughout Canada and the United States. We liked the idea, so Petr got a black powder gun — a copy, of course, not an original. I sewed old-fashioned shirts for Petr and Tom. They made their hats and tried their luck in the shooting competitions. Tom was tireless in throwing knife and tomahawk. He also used his homemade bow and proudly aimed his arrows, gaining admiration from the other boys. The "Rendez-vous" inspired us in another project, to make our own teepee. Many participants used teepees instead of tents; some had them nicely decorated. We tried sleeping in one and liked it very much, as it was more airy than a tent. Petr got an old outfitter's tent and he cut a teepee from it. The size was about half that of the original, but it was enough for two to sleep in. Then Petr and both children sewed it by hand. That same summer, Kate and Tom used it for their own camping. We found a place close to Canmore, where they could set up their teepee. Not too far away, so we could visit them, but not too close, so they avoided unwelcome visitors. Kate and Tom lived there for a week and tasted an independent life. Of course, Cir was with them. We visited them every day and brought supplies. However, what they cooked, how they organized their days, how they arranged the interior of the teepee, was their own responsibility. They both liked it very much, so they camped this way on some future holidays. Once, they were close to the Bow River and had a small kayak with them. Of course, I worried but they managed everything perfectly. Only a mother of Tom's friend, who lived on the other side of the river, told me with some concern, how Tom surprised them. He had come to visit and when they accompanied him back to the river, he proudly got into his kayak and paddled back on the still high river.

As seasonal workers, Petr and I were not eligible for holidays. In this year the World Fair, Expo 1986, opened in Vancouver. Already, years ago in Montreal, the Czech exposition had been very successful and highly publicized in Czechoslovakia. We had seen some TV and film shots and read reports, but it looked so far away, as if from another planet. Now a similar exposition was so close, just a day of driving! It was very tempting for us, even to see Vancouver, the city by the Pacific surrounded by mountains. Finally, we made an arrangement with our employers and took a week off in September. We also hoped that with the summer holidays over, Expo would not be so crowded. However, the same idea occurred to thousands of other people and visitors' records were set in September.

We again loaded our camper and, with joyful expectations, set out to the west. Even though it was just a holiday trip, it was a kind of closure to our wandering through Canada, always in the direction of the Pacific. British Columbia really is "super natural" as their advertising says. We drove through the mountain passes and valleys and worried if our old pick-up truck would last. It already showed the marks of age and use, but it still managed this trip. We met, in Vancouver, my other friend from the Czech university. It was very nice to have a friend in Vancouver! Even though our visit coincided with his move to Victoria, he showed us the city and helped us with accommodations which, at the time of Expo, were very expensive. We bought a three-day pass for the fair and from that moment on, at nearly each pavillion, we had to stand in line. We laughed as it was the first time since we left Czechoslovakia that we had to wait in lines. Back in our old country, we lined up for everything and people there accepted it as a way of life. In Canada, nobody was used to waiting, but at Expo there was no choice. However, we liked it all very much. The theme "transportation" was, for our children, very relevant. The vivid exhibition of different kinds of transportation using water, land and air, was done very well and each section had some highlights. There was a restored boat from the seventeenth century, now open for sightseeing, a display of the evolution of planes, which included the oldest "flying machines" and balloons, and car salons which showed the oldest cars to the newest futuristic models. Some pavillions showed automatic miniatures of traffic; probably the best was in the Japan pavillion. The Swiss pavillion had a humourous display showing the path taken by a ping-pong ball through a complex mechanized maze. This was great fun and the children did not want to leave. However, the highlight for Kate and Tom was the Expo Robot. They had looked forward to it and they were not disappointed, as the Robot talked to them and answered questions. Even we adults were surprised, when in the middle of a sentence, the Robot said to Tom, "I guess you should turn. Your father would like to take a picture."

Only in the Czech pavilion, we felt uncomfortable and decided to speak in English. We discussed with Kate and Tom, each evening, what we saw, what each of us liked most and what awoke our interest. We found the best time for talking was when we waited for the daily fireworks, which closed the exhibition, or as we strolled along the Pacific, which was another a new experience for all of us.

On our way back, we drove through the Okanagan Valley which is known for its fruit. As it was fall, we visited a "u-pick" orchard and picked a couple of boxes of apples and pears for just a few dollars. Another big experience on our trip occurred when we stopped at Salmon Arm for a short rest and walked by the river. Suddenly, we realized it was a salmon run! So many times we had read about it and suddenly we saw it with our own eyes. Salmon — big, small, some already completely red, some only partly, some already with their upper jaw bent into a hook. We ran along the river and never tired of watching. I really could not say, which was a bigger experience for me, Expo or the salmon run.

17
Canadian Citizens

*"Perhaps I had found a country which has the right size of popu-
lation so that it is an extended village. You don't get lost in it,
except geographically. I was also attracted by the fact that ours
is a country whose history lies in the future, a place where one
can have hope."* — John C. Polanyi

I had to wind up my seasonal Forestry job with a written report
describing both projects, our activities and the results, and including a
proposal for next year. My co-worker had ended the season earlier to
attend school, so I had to do the report alone. To be confident of my
English writing, I read the report with my friend, who had been giving
me English lessons. However, I was still mortified when a secretary,
who was to retype the report, started to scream that she did not
understand it and she would not type it. I was glad that the District
Forest Officer did not have such an attitude! He took my report, asked
me a couple of questions, changed some sentences and in ten minutes
the problems were solved. Yet, I was always worried afterwards,
about how my reports would be received.

In the fall, our family had an important anniversary. We had been in
Canada for three years and, by law, we could now apply for Canadian
citizenship. Frankly, we could hardly wait to obtain it! Even with
"Landed Immigrant" status we did not feel very safe, as if we really
did not fit anywhere. Our passports, our most important documents,
were legal only for travel to Yugoslavia and only for a fixed period, so
they were already invalid. We still had Czech citizenship, but we
could not count that, as it was subject to changes in the political
situation. In addition, according to Czech law, we had committed an
offence and would be jailed if we returned. Truly, we did not think
about returning at all, and we never regretted our departure. Despite
some difficulties and problems with work, we always appreciated life
in Canada. It had something that our old country could not offer us,
freedom. Canada had liberty of human expression as well as abundant
free space. We hoped that the first kind of freedom would come to
Czechoslovakia, one day. The second kind, the free space, one could
not find in overcrowded Europe any more. And we appreciated this
kind of freedom very much. We had hoped to find it when we decided

on our new country and we were happy that our expectations were realized. For this reason, right after the three-year waiting period in Canada had passed, we applied for citizenship.

While we waited for the response to our applications, I found that my surname was a source of confusion. In Czech, women's surnames usually ended with "-ova" which means female. Here in Canada, I had a problem to explain why my surname differed from Petr's. We were even asked if we were married. Kate had already decided, on her own, to use the surname without "-ova." However, we both had to officially apply for a change. It took more time than we expected, so Kate and I had the interview and took the oath for Canadian citizenship two months later than Petr and Tom. We studied before the interviews and tried to expand our knowledge about Canadian history, geography, and politics. The interviews went without any problems. I even talked about my unusual wedding ring as I have an elk tooth (it is considered a trophy in Europe and is used in hunting jewelry) inserted in the ring. It was great to talk in English, without much difficulty. What a difference from the interview three and half years ago at the immigration office!

The actual Canadian citizenship oaths were, for us, festive moments. We dressed in our best; I even wore a dress I had specially made for this occasion. As Petr and I took our oaths separately, we experienced it twice. We all drove in, both times, together. Both occasions were similar — a group of twenty to thirty people, young and older, had ten to thirteen different origins. Some spoke fluently, some with broken English, but all declared solemnly, and ceremonially, their loyalty to our new country, Canada. I could say, speaking for our family, we meant every word and we proudly accepted the documents of our new nationality, and the congratulations of the citizenship officials.

We celebrated by indulging in a luxury — we went out for lunch. Back in Canmore, we stopped at the benchlands to take some pictures with a huge Canadian flag and, of course, mountains in the background.

The following winter, I stayed home. Even if I had found a job in town, the money would have been the same as my Unemployment Insurance payments. It was very comfortable to stay home and devote time to my family and my hobbies. However, we did not save a penny.

As we met more people in Canmore, we found that many had moved to the town due to their love of the mountains. Some had a very humble lifestyle. They lived, as we say in Czech, "from hand to mouth." However, they preferred to enjoy life, to have beautiful experiences in the mountains rather than to accumulate possessions and to be depending on money. We were happy to find we were not so unusual, for moving to a place that we liked, without the assurance of a job. The "proper" way was usually the opposite, as most people moved because they had found a job.

The communist regime, where we came from, had a different approach to work. Work was not only everybody's privilege, which was often stressed, but also one's duty. Persons without a job were, in fact, prosecuted. Unemployment did not exist, but nobody could take time off for hobbies, a longer holiday, or travelling either. The average citizen had only two to four weeks of time off each year and travelling was very restricted. As I mentioned before, it was a long and difficult process to get a permit to travel abroad. Only a privileged few at the top of the communist party heirarchy got access to trips to foreign countries. The rest of us could only dream about it; and to dream about what we would like to do, if we didn't need to go to work each day. When we fled from Czechoslovakia, our situation changed. Suddenly, we did not need to go to work, but often wished we could, if only we could find a job! On the other hand, we had free time and it was up to us what to do with it. We often heard other people complain how they were restricted because of a lack of money, so they could not do what they wanted. Of course, money permits more choices, but I disagree that it is necessary for independence and happiness. The motivation must come from inside of each individual. Money does not help if one lacks inspiration, a zest to do something, joy for living, or a deep appreciation of the nature around us.

Our first years were very "lean," concerning income, but this did not spoil our happiness and we always found a hobby. It was not a big task to find something of interest in the mountains. We only wondered about people, who had moved to Canmore without any feeling for the surroundings, just a vision of good investments or better profits. Unfortunately, it seemed that as Canmore grew, these newcomers predominated.

Our friend Don was a living example of our theories. To realize his projects and to reach his objectives, he needed almost no money. He possessed will, courage, and zest. His ski trip from Calgary to the Pacific, which he made a couple of years later, probably best illustrates this. He travelled alone and took only a small pack-sack, not even a tent. Several times, he had to interrupt his trip, only to start again later at the same spot. He went through a number of ridges and valleys, experienced all kinds of weather, including heavy snowfalls, freezing rain, fog, and heavy frosts as well as calm, beautiful days with sunshine and nights full of stars. When he came to small villages and hamlets, he met different kinds of people, but mostly nobody in the mountains. Several times, he met wolves, and once he was worried by the encounter, but nothing happened. He had to ski through deep snow and, later, to carry his skis because of a lack of snow. In fact, he started his trip carrying his skis and he also finished it in this way. The last seventy kilometres to the coast was snow free, but Don finished the trip according to his plan. On the shores of the Pacific, he put the skis on and entered the ocean. For such a trip, money was nearly worthless, other human qualities were needed. Don's highest expenses on the trip were probably his telephone bills to contact his family. From time to time, he called us and told us about his progress. With a thrill, we waited for his information and we "lived" the trip through Don's descriptions.

Our life did not include such big adventures, but we enjoyed our own outings, observing wildlife and even some hunting. A few times we went to south-eastern Alberta to hunt antelope. In winter, cross-country skiing took most of our leisure time.We did not even need to leave town as that winter, 1987, the Canmore Nordic Centre, the focus for nordic disciplines during the 1988 Winter Olympics, was already finished. It was thrilling to live in a town which would be a part of the Olympic games, especially for our preferred sport, though cross-country skiing did not yet have the popularity it would attain later.

Kate and Tom had tried different sports. When we discussed which sport to pursue with them, Petr suggested cross-country skiing to work on their technique. They usually skiied with us and it would be better to know proper technique. The nordic club in Canmore also had a children's program, called Jackrabbits. The name was taken from an enthusiastic Norwegian skier, who had moved to Canada and actively promoted cross-country skiing, especially for children. "Jackrabbit" Johannsen lived a healthy life for 103 years.

At the time, there were about twenty Canmore children involved in the program. (A few years later, the numbers jumped to 140.) In this sport, our children were not beginners, as in other sports. They both caught up quickly with the other children, moving ahead and even entering their first races. Kate and Tom liked the program, and we were happy that the kids had found "their" sport. At this time, we had no idea that this sport would eventually lead them to the national teams. Of course, that took several more years. For now, we all learned, including Petr, who tried to renew his coaching skills, gained some twenty years ago. I helped to organize races and we had a chance to see how competition was organized in preparation for the 1988 Olympics.

Christmas drew near, with the usual household preparations, as well as the commercial emphasis in the shops. Festive decorations adorned shop windows, malls, banks and offices, with a thousand lights, inside and out. The Christmas rush seemed to start, already, in November with carols on radio and TV and ads for all kinds of goods that would be the best and right Christmas gifts. People asked each other if they were ready for the holidays. I was shocked to hear this question in November. Naturally, our best memories are from the time when our children were small. Their expectations, impatience and joy were the best reward for our Christmas preparations. When they outgrew the belief that gifts are distributed by the Christ-child, a tradition in our old country, both Kate and Tom geared up for presenting gifts to others. Our family believed that the best gifts are handmade ones. It is easier to buy something than to make it, a process needing time to think and to do the work. So Christmas gifts involved secret production, behind closed doors, followed by joy under the Christmas tree. This was a little at odds with ads and the shopping fever around us.

Most of the celebration happened before the holidays and it was not an exception to see Christmas trees thrown away on December 26. Many Christmas decorations did not survive New Year. We had grown up in a tradition, where most celebrations occurred after December 24, when families and friends visited each other. Here in Canada, we did not have any family, so we tried to find the best way to use the feast time. The question was, what to do next, when supper was consumed, the lights on the Christmas tree lit, the carols were sung, and the gifts given? For our family, as I have mentioned, the biggest celebration was on Christmas Eve, which we finished by attending midnight mass. Then we had two beautiful days, when everything was done, the food cooked and the days just waiting to be enjoyed. Very soon, we found that Christmas Day is an excellent time for skiing as not many people are out.

I thought it would be fun to spend a couple of days in a mountain cabin. Of course, I did not think of using an expensive one, where the price included meals, but about finding a cabin where we could cook for ourselves. I booked the Alpine Club of Canada's hut at Lake O'Hara and I presented the stay to my family as one of my gifts. The Lake O'Hara area is well known to hikers and has eighty kilometres of trails with specular views of more than a dozen lakes and ponds and the ragged peaks of the continental divide. The days I booked were around New Year's day. The hut was fully occupied, a little noisy each evening, and the parties changed daily. However, it was very enjoyable. There was a lot of snow, so we could do trips in any direction. The nights were cold and clear, with a full moon that illuminated the nearby mountain tops with colors from light blue to pink. It was very beautiful, especially around the lake. Even when temperatures dropped below - 30° Celsius, we did not miss a chance for night skiing on the lake. Since then, it has become our Christmas tradition to spend time at some cabin. On Christmas Day is best, as the huts are nearly empty then.

Cir accompanied us on our trips whenever we could take him. He was always very obedient and stayed by our heels even when we were on skis. Often he had to run fast on the down hills and go slowly up hills. However, he never stepped in front of us and we never had any problem with him. In his early years, Cir showed joy and impatience whenever Petr took out his pack-sack and gun and was always ready to go out. Now Cir's reaction changed, when he saw us take our skis. He was very sad, whenever we loft him at home.

One morning we found that he moved very slowly. By evening, he was nearly paralyzed and unable to take a single step on his own. We had to carry him to see a veterinarian in Canmore. Unfortunately, she could not find anything, but recommended a deep X-ray in case there was a spinal problem. We could not agree with her. Cir had never before showed any sign of pain or difficulty in hiking with us over long distances. We called a Czech veterinarian in Calgary and he made some guesses: poison — we excluded it, somebody had hit him — also impossible. He called again at night, still thinking about it, and asked if Cir had gotten his yearly shot against distemper. He considered it a trivial question, but unfortunately, this was the reason for Cir's paralysis. When we came to Canada, we were told about the needed shots in Ontario, where only one lifetime shot against distemper is given. We did not know it was different in Alberta, where this quickly-spreading disease had literally killed one third of the cat population and also affected dogs. For this reason, yearly vaccination was recommended. Our trailer park just swarmed with cats so it was probably easy for Cir to catch the deadly disease. The worst was yet to come, as there was no medicine available. We were told that young animals usually do not survive. However, Cir was a very strong adult, so we hoped he could recover. His strong appetite definitely helped him. He was not able to eat solid food, but he still enjoyed milk or light soup, which probably saved his life. The disease usually dehydrates animals and they die. Cir was unable to move for some days. Any time he tried to stand up and showed discomfort we carried him outside on a blanket (Cir weighed about thirty-eight kilos!). He then crawled ahead a little, made his business and we carried him back in. A few days passed and Cir tried to lift himself on his front legs and to take some steps. It looked like he was drunk, but it was progress. After a while, he started to walk, but he tired quickly. However, we were very, very happy.

When he stabilized and was again in as good shape as before the illness, we took him to Calgary for a shot. The veterinarian congratulated us because not many dogs survive the disease. However, some symptoms of the illness remained. After long hikes, especially on rocky terrain, the paralysis in Cir's rear legs sometimes came back. He had to rest, or even completely stop the trip. As he aged, it became worse until he was not able to do long trips any more. However, by this time he was already thirteen years old, so he was entitled to rest.

18
Winter Olympic Games 1988

"The XV Olympic Winter Games of 1988 will never be forgotten. No other single event has ever generated such enthusiasm, energy and pride in Albertans, and indeed in Canadians." — Don R. Getty

Spring became the traditional time for our vacations. As we both worked over the summers and Petr also over the winters, we used the spring breaks in our childrens' schooling for travelling. It meant we had to go either south to the USA, or west to the coast. We would have loved to see Canada's north, but it was still winter there. Later, when Kate and Tom's racing season lasted until the spring break, we had to excuse them from school to take our holidays as we were determined not to miss these shared, family experiences. I was always surprised to hear how other people went on holiday without their children. They usually explained that their children had different interests than the parents. Maybe this would be so when the children grew older, but so far we did not even think to ask them. We just said, we would like to go to such a place, where we could see so and so. Afterwards, we planned the trip with maps and our children happily joined in. It was the same with other activities.

In the spring of 1987, we wanted to use our new Canadian passports, because we were so proud to have them. We used the invitation of my school friend, presently living in Victoria. He shared a cottage near Mt. Baker, in Washington, and he had invited us to spend a couple of days with him. Before we reached the American border, I nervously prepared our passports, anticipating difficulties at the border. To my surprise, the customs officers were not interested in them at all! They just asked a few questions and let us go.

In this year, even though I had again been promised a job from Forestry, I waited until late June to start work. I worked with the same young woman as in the previous year, on another mountain pine beetle project covering two locations. Besides the Bow District, we worked in the south of the province, around Crowsnest Pass. We stayed there overnight but still made high mileage. The most southern part of the Crowsnest District borders on Waterton National Park. From time to time, a grizzly crossed the park boundary and ranged on the adjacent leased land. It happened again when we were working there. Unfortunately, the bear was a killer, and attacked cattle. According to one report, six cows were killed within a couple of weeks. However, the Forestry Office had not informed us about this. The summer was wet, so we could not drive near some of our plots. Once, as we walked in, some considerable distance, we met a group of armed ranchers. They were enormously surprised to see us walking unarmed in the area, where they did not dare to ride horses alone and always carried a gun. On our next visit, we found some of our bait pulled down from the trees. The claw marks evoked respect, even a shudder. We were glad that we did not meet the bear.

The work finished after three months — not enough to claim Unemployment Insurance benefits, so I had to find some winter work. As before, this was not easy. Finally, I had to take a cleaning job in a hotel. The hours were irregular; sometimes I worked only a few hours a day. I was fortunate that the local elementary school was looking for a lunch-hour supervisor. I applied, and got the job, and the experience of numerous short runs: to the hotel, to school, to the hotel, then home. And because life is not always simple, at the same time Petr lost his job. What he found next was only short term.

It was not easy for us, but we did not have much time to mourn about it. The final preparations for the upcoming Olympic Winter Games in Calgary were under way. One could feel the thrill and enthusiasm for the big event. Even people in Canmore, with little or no knowledge about nordic sports, wanted detailed information and tried to join in the event. The organizing committee had no problem finding volunteers, as there were many times the number actually needed, but it was hard work to select suitable people. I went to one interview for hosts and translators. The hall was completely full, the chance of getting a position one to ten. I did not make it, due to my still imperfect English.

For the 1988 Olympic Winter Games, the torch bearing also attracted a huge quantity of applications. The organizers wanted to promote the "Olympic feeling" in the whole country, so it was decided that before the torch would reach Calgary, it would cross through most of Canada. A detailed plan, with defined sections, was announced and volunteers sent in applications for each section. The number of applications, from children, adults and citizens of advanced age, far surpassed expectations. Occasionally, known athletes got first choice, but mostly the draw decided who would run with the torch. Kate applied unsuccessfully for a couple of sections. Of course, we did not know that some people had applied for many sections.

Tom made it to a selection for a childrens' dance in the Opening Ceremonies. A group of twenty-four children was chosen from Banff and Canmore. From the start, Tom was "bored" as only a few local boys were chosen. After they started rehearsals in Calgary, he found there were more boys and was very proud of his achievement.

Petr was chosen as a van driver. He drove for two months, sometimes locally, in Canmore, sometimes to Calgary. For the duration of the competition, he was selected to drive for the Russian team, probably due to his knowledge of Slavic languages. It was a little ironic in the light of our escape, but in this top-level sporting event, political problems were mostly suppressed. I nearly signed on as a volunteer in another area, but then I realized that somebody had to work to support our family. We both could not afford to work as volunteers on a full-time basis. I regretted the missed opportunity none-the-less. Each hotel tried hard to keep their own personnel because the volunteer work drew away the available workers. I stayed with the hotel, and with my other job in the local school. During the Olympic games, the school gave students time off to watch the big event and, actually, many teachers and older students worked as volunteers. My lunch-time supervision job ended, but I did supervision (and cleaning) for athletes who were billetted in our school and helping with the games as forerunners (skiers who ski a race course in advance of the races to ensure that the first racers are not placed at a disadvantage by being the first to ski a track that may be rough or slow due to crusty or fresh snow). For my small part, I volunteered to chaperone and help with with costumes at the childrens' rehearsals in Calgary for the Opening Ceremonies.

All around us the Olympic preparations culminated, overshadowing all other happenings. All citizens of the Bow Valley were invited to an opening of the new down-hill centre at Nakiska. The building of the centre was preceded by many discussions and disputes about the location. On the west side of Calgary, right by Highway 1, a new Olympic Centre was built, with ski jumps and track for bobsled and luge. Within the city, new arenas were built for speed skating, hockey, and figure skating. The Calgary "Saddledome" became known for its unique architecture, the roof design being reminiscent of an equestrian saddle. In the city centre, a place was set up for medal presentations.

This Olympic Plaza became the most visited area during the games. Thousands of spectators came each evening for medal presentation and there was not enough room for everybody. The plaza was busy not only in the evenings, but throughout the day, when it became a destination for visitors, spectators and collectors, who came to exchange Olympic pins. According to Canadian tradition, representatives of minorities living in Canada were invited to open booths around Olympic Plaza to sell ethnic food and souvenirs. The Czech organization in Calgary asked Kate to help. She spent a week, in the middle of the Olympic rush, helping in the booth. She was even dressed in Czech folk costume.

Of course, we were mostly focussed on the Canmore Nordic Centre, which was built for the 1988 Olympic Winter Games. The building of ski trails started in 1986. The next year, the centre hosted international races to fulfill pre-Olympic requirements. At this time, we met the Czech Biathlon Team, who found themselves in a somewhat complicated situation. They had stayed a few days after the World Cup was over, but they had no transportation. The socialist countries never had any extra money, so they could not rent a car and the organizers of the World Cup provided transportation just for the duration of the races. At this time, all athletes from socialist countries had strict orders not to meet with any escapees. When we learned of their situation, we went to the hotel and offered to let them use our truck (we now had a newer one, more reliable). Orders or not — they gladly accepted our offer but did not yet find the courage to visit us. Not until later, after the Olympics, when I worked as a hostess for the Czech team during another World Cup, did the tension begin to ease, due to the changing situation behind the Iron Curtain.

During the Olympics, we, of course, did not have any idea about the future, so politics were "taboo" for athletes and also for hosts. Petr, due to his driving, also met the Czech team, but only a few people talked to him. The fear of being seen with an emigrant was very strong.

In the late fall, before the games, the mountains received heavy snowfalls. However, as usual, the venues at the Canmore Nordic Centre and at Nakiska had only moderate accumulations of snow and the range of the snow-making equipment was limited. However, the organizers packed the trails at both venues with snow brought in by truck. All Olympic venues, including Calgary, relied on their snow-making equipment, but the foundation of natural snow which could also be spread on an extended area was welcome. The Olympics benefitted from the forward-thinking decision. In the second week, the Chinook, the warm wind from the Pacific, boosted temperatures to between +14° and +17° Celsius. However, no races were postponed or cancelled. There was still enough snow.

After the New Year, the nordic centre was closed to the public, including members of ski clubs. As Kate and Tom did not want to abandon their ski training, we had to find a substitute place for skiing. We choose a meadow by the road to Spray Lakes, about twenty minutes of driving from Canmore. With the help of friends, a trail was made, and I acquired another duty, to pick up Tom and Kate, sometimes with their friends, after school and give them a ride for training and back. Tom was also signed up for competition in Nordic Combined, a combination of skiing and ski-jumping. So far, we drove to Banff for training in ski-jumping. However, as the number of rehearsals for the Opening Ceremonies increased, he had less and less time for this training. Fortunately, he was a good skier so what he lost in races on ski-jumps, he regained through skiing. Unfortunately, his club did not train in the summer and afterwards, they moved completely to Calgary. This forced Tom to change his sport. He decided for biathlon, as due to the Olympic Games, this sport had caught Tom's attention. Kate stayed with cross-country skiing for a while.

Canmore gained a sports complex due to the Olympic games, housing a new curling facility and a swimming pool. Both were added to the existing recreation centre, which had a hockey rink. The enlarged facility was used as an "Olympic village," with accommodation for 600 athletes and coaches. Right beside it was another large building, where the volunteer centre was located. From here, volunteers could start their shifts, receive information, relax or eat, check the results of competitions, or watch the races on television.

In January, Canmore streets were decorated with flags and banners illustrating Olympic Winter Games motifs. The banners were the projects of school children in Tom's classes, so our household had helped to make three of the flags. Tom was very proud, as one of his flags remained in the school gymnasium after the Olympics, as a permanent decoration. The annual Canmore Winter Festival at the end of January focussed on the coming big event. Some side streets were closed to traffic, becoming walking zones, and were decorated with ice sculptures. The ice-sculpture competition was an annual event in Canmore, but it was necessary to have as many participants as possible. Again, the answer was to involve school children. Even though the results were not professional, the children enjoyed participating and contributing to the festive atmosphere in town. Both our children tried their artistic skills: Kate and some other girls made a piano, Tom created a walrus. Actually, his sculpture turned out very well, and this inspired Tom to join in the ice sculpture competitions in future years.

One week before the beginning of the Olympic Winter Games, there was an official rehearsal for the opening. As parents of a participant, we got free tickets. We liked the rehearsal very much, even though we did not experience the "real" ceremony where spectators were given specific colorful covers, so the audience looked like Olympic rings. On the other hand, we had first-hand experience of the shaking of the just-completed seating as we sat and vibrated with each stormy round of applause and foot-stamping. We suspected that the organizers wanted to test the stability of the structures prior to the event itself. However, it was a magnificent performance, and we were glad of the opportunity to view it.

Immediately after the official Opening Ceremonies in Calgary, the Olympic torch was carried to the Canmore Nordic Centre. For most of the distance, it travelled by car until just before Canmore. Then came the most festive moment for Canmore residents: the Olympic torch was passed from hand to hand until it reached the nordic centre. Most of the people, who lined the Canmore streets, carried candles, which they lit from the Olympic flame. The local photo-lab made pictures, so nearly everybody had a souvenir of the moment.

The organizers expected that the Olympic flame would reach the nordic centre in two hours. However, it took almost five, as nearly everybody who was able to walk came to take part. Natives from the Stoney Indian Reservation drummed and waited in their ceremonial costumes near the town limits. In the streets were families with small children, local organizations, and bands. Buses transported patients and staff from the hospital and the local seniors' lodge. Despite the long wait, nobody left, and nobody was angry. People talked to friends as well as to strangers, made jokes, and laughed. When finally we got a chance to touch the torch and pass it down the line, everybody beamed. Afterwards, most of us hurried up to the Canmore

Nordic Centre. Those who were fast enough could see the end of the "torch passing" and witness the ceremonial lighting of the Olympic flame at the centre. The last spots in line, before the flame reached the Olympic dish, were reserved for the children participating in the Opening Ceremonies. They came directly from Calgary, dressed in their blue and silver costumes and proudly moved through Canmore like young celebrities. The large tent, with refreshment booths for the spectators, was lit long into the night and vibrated with life.

The next day, the Opening Ceremonies took place at the Canmore Nordic Centre. Unfortunately, my only chance to see this or most of the competitions was to steal glances at the TV while working in the hotel or to watch the evening broadcasts. The rest of my family was more fortunate. Both children attended most of the competitions at the nordic centre. Kate, of course, spent some days working in Calgary. Petr also saw most of the races because he drove athletes or officials to the nordic centre or to competitions in Calgary.

I will never forget the atmosphere of the races which I did have the chance to see. It was the same feeling as with the torch passing: joy, admiration of the sport, good will among the people. The groups of fans from different countries supported their athletes not only with cheering, but they also waved flags (the largest were the best) and rang bells. Everybody was infected with a common mood of happiness. Many times, I remembered the Olympic motto from ancient times, "Give people bread and the games." Surely, as in Greek or Roman times, the games filled the subconscious mind of the people, eroded their differences, and increased their admiration for the sports competitors and their achievements.

The weather was on the side of the games. The blue Alberta sky was nearly cloudless making each day sunny and warm, actually too warm for the winter races, but no competition was cancelled. When, after two weeks, it was time for the Closing Ceremonies and the Olympic flame slowly went down at the nordic centre and at the Calgary Tower, we all felt a sadness. Our time of big excitement was over.

After the Olympics, there were meetings, mostly to thank the volunteers for their work. We attended a couple. They were nice, but life went on, leaving just pleasant memories. By the way, due to the Olympic organization and the huge response of volunteers, the XV Olympic Winter Games in Calgary did not finish with the usual deficit, but with a profit.

Welcome to Alberta.

Hiking in the Rockies.

Kate towered above her sports mates.

Cir.

- 173 -

Talking to the robot at Expo 1986 in Vancouver.

Winter camping.

Canadian citizens!

Don and Tom,
top of Third Sister.

Tom passes the Olympic torch at
the opening of the 1988 Olympics.

Tom and Kate, medalists at the
Canadian Championships 1993.

Petr in the Yukon.

Petr's sister with
Tom in
Drumheller

19
Petr's Work in the Yukon

"My home is a tent — floor is of grass — grub varies at times
My book is nature — each day but a page
My music the breeze through the pines." — author unknown.

The work situation was particularly hard for us in 1988. Forestry let me know that they would have no seasonal summer jobs. Petr had not worked since January. Hotels were half empty after the Olympic Games, or rather business had returned to normal with fluctuating numbers of visitors. I never knew ahead of time how many hours I would work. Of course, I still hoped to use my training and education rather than staying with my job at the hotel. Unfortunately, so far my applications to Alberta and British Columbia forestry employers were either not answered at all, or politely "put on file." I also applied to parks departments, both federal and provincial. I succeeded only in becoming a seasonal campground attendant with Banff National Park. The term of employment was just a little longer than the summer holidays.

Petr had started, in the winter, to correspond with an outfitter from the Yukon. The idea to be a hunting guide in the north was very attractive to Petr and he wanted to try this job, at least for a while. When, after the Olympic Games, Petr again contacted the outfitter, he offered him a job beginning at the end of April. The Yukon government, in view of a high bear population, had opened a spring hunting season for grizzly bears around Whitehorse. Petr wrote later that they often saw, in a relatively small area, about ten to fifteen grizzlies, an unusual number. So, at the end of April, Petr said good-bye to us and drove north. I knew it was his dream since boyhood and he was glad to have a chance to try it. It was also work, even if not highly paid, and would last, at least, for half of a year. However, Petr was leaving at a time when our financial reserves were minimal and I did not yet know if I would find a job. So even with the best will, I could not share his enthusiasm.

It meant, for me, to clench my teeth, to go on in hope that we would survive, and to enjoy the small pleasures which life offered. In time, we looked forward Petr's letters and his accounts of the area, his wilderness observations and stories of hunts which we, ourselves, were not able to experience. It was definitely not an easy job, Petr's work in the north. It needed physical and moral strength to live in a virtual wilderness, to take care of the guests, and manage the work fairly. From time to time, I found, in Petr's letters, the unspoken words about tiredness and loneliness in the huge northern wilderness. In this mood, Petr was willing to confess some mistakes from the past, which he regretted. Our children were shocked. They took their strict father as a matter of course and were not used his apologies for anything. On the other hand, Petr's job, though demanding, gave him many chances to "make memories," as we say in Czech.

Later, Petr described this time to his friends with these words:

"My youthful dream — to see the wilderness of the north — came into being when I contacted Rick, an outfitter from the Yukon. He called me in April, asking if I could start. I did not have any job, so Eva agreed. The wage was not high, but I was able to send everything home, as I did not need any money in the wilderness.

It is about 2,700 kilometres from Canmore to Whitehorse, and over half of the way I drove on the Alaska highway. I took along some stuff for Rick — a stove, saddles, and salt for the horses, etcetera, and on April 20 I set out, through Banff and Jasper to Prince George. I saw the beautiful Mount Robson for the first time. From Prince George, I drove to Fort St. John, and then through mostly uninhabited areas to Fort Nelson. From there, the highway went between two small mountains and over the Liard River to the first Yukon town, Watson Lake. Another 450 kilometres went through a vast land, where only single families lived around gas stations, to the Yukon's capital, Whitehorse. The whole Yukon Territory has about 25,000 residents, and nearly 19,000 live in Whitehorse. I thought of the Gold Rush, when about 30,000 people lived in Dawson City, and Whitehorse was just a small settlement. Today, Dawson has only about 600 inhabitants. The clean creeks and rivers always remind me of the search for gold and, I found later, some people still try their luck. It was already spring when I reached Whitehorse. The tops of the surrounding hills were still white with snow, the Yukon River was muddy, but the days were warm and above all, long. Sunrise was at about 5:00 a.m., sunset about 10:30 p.m., and each day, the days grew longer.

My time in the Yukon was divided into three parts: the spring bear hunt, the preparation for the main season, and the main hunting season. The spring hunt was north-west from Bennett Lake, about forty minutes flying time from Whitehorse. The landscape was composed of barren hills with scattered groves around creeks and lakes. We built a camp in one of the side valleys, which was about five kilometres long. It was the only place where the plane was able to land. We saw several moose there and, in the end of the valley, many Dall sheep. According to previous observations, the occurrence of bears was high there, with one exceptionally huge grizzly. The most time, in our three-week bear hunt, was spent in patient observation of our surroundings from some good survey point. Our guests got three grizzly and two black bears. The days were long, dawn came right after midnight. The bears were hungry after their winter sleep and they criss-crossed the country for the whole twenty-four hours of each day. They searched for winter kills and also for first greens, dry berries or dug out roots. They looked for newborn lambs and moose calves. In later years I saw, many times, how desperately a moose cow tries to hide with her newborn calf, ahead of a grizzly.

The preparation for the main season started in Whitehorse, where we fixed and made many necessities for the outfit. Actually, all equipment must be checked and repaired completely before the season. We worked on the plane and repaired rubber boats and quads. We mended saddles and reins, tents and camp equipment and did lots of painting. The outfitter bought several new horses and we had to break three of them. Unfortunately, one could not be used for a whole season, as he was hard to break, and we did not have enough time for it. I also made four portable showers, which run on electric power from a generator and are heated by propane. In the season, propane was widely used for cooking and lighting, which saved our time. During the preparations, I had opportunities take some time off and visit historic places around Bennett Lake, from where the gold seekers during the rush made rafts and boats and floated down the Yukon River to Dawson City. From Bennett Lake, it is not far to the Pacific Ocean, travelling through Alaska. The other interesting place is Haines Junction, a town on the edge of Kluane National Park, the site of one of the world's largest glaciers.

When we had everything ready for the season, we had to move the horses to the main camp. At the start of July, we drove the horses to the last town, Elsa. From there, we had to ride as there was no road from Elsa to the main camp. After a half day of preparation, packing and saddling the horses for a three-day trip, we finally set off at six o'clock in the evening. There were four of us. Bill led us, because he knew the way. I was in the middle, Cody in the back, and Sunny moved around and herded back the loose horses. All of us, except Sunny, led one pack horse behind us on a six-metre-long rope. The rest of the horses were loose, as it would be impractical in such terrain to tie them together. We rode for about eight hours without stopping. Then we made camp for the night. Unfortunately, this was just before I lost my horse. He had been extensively ridden just before our trip, which was too much for such a young horse. He started to limp and then suddenly collapsed. There was no way to help him. Sunny shot him and left the carcass for wolves and bears. The next day we rode twelve hours without stopping. We started at 10:00 in the morning and just before noon, Bill's horse and his packhorse fell into a swamp. They were lucky and got out unhurt. I was about fifty metres behind them and unable to help Bill. In one moment, I did not see Bill at all, as his horse had pushed him down. When Bill and the horses finally got up, we still had to cross the Beaver River. Here, I involuntarily went into the water and Bill followed, when our horses lost their balance in the mud on the shore as they were coming out of the water. We did not stop to rest and after three hours of riding, our clothes were dry. We made camp after midnight and continued on the next day, with four hours riding to Carpenter Lake. We stayed there for ten days before we moved the horses to the main camp. Altogether, we rode 110 kilometres through beautiful wild country and enjoyed gorgeous weather. One thing was funny — after a couple of days we completely lost count of time, I guess due to long days with daylight lasting until midnight. After our arrival at Carpenter Lake, we expected to see a pilot, who would fly me back to Whitehorse. We were a little upset, when he did not show up until the next day. It turned out that the pilot was on time but we had somehow added a day to our trip calculations. From Whitehorse, I flew home for a short visit, as I had an interview for a forestry job. Unfortunately, I was not successful.

On my way back, I flew through Vancouver. Again the weather was beautiful, so I saw a big part of British Columbia from the air. From Whitehorse, I drove 500 kilometres back to Elsa. For a part of the way, I drove along the Yukon River, which leads to Dawson City. I passed the famous Five Fingers Rapids, then the Pelly and Steward Rivers, another town, Mayo, and finally came to Elsa. Rick picked me up with his small plane at a lake and we landed on Elliot Lake, one of his base camps. The other guide and I had to clean and prepare everything for the upcoming season there and at another base camp by Warm Lake. We had to chop enough firewood to last through the hunting season, which is not easy on the tundra. We had to level all the cabins and tent bases, because they were lifted and shifted due to winter frost. We also put canvas roofs on the guest cabins and tents, fixed, cleaned, painted and did other odd jobs, seemingly without end, even with twenty hours of daylight to do the work.

At the end of July, we loaded two Honda ATVs and other equipment into a big float plane and flew to another camp which was named "Tom-Tom." From there I and the other guide, Mike, set off on a trip to Small Wind River and Royal Creek, a distance of about 150 kilometres. The whole trip was through wilderness, with no trail at all. Besides our personal equipment such as a tent, sleeping bags and food, we carried tools for levelling and building airstrips for plane landing on gravel bars around the mentioned watercourses. The description of the trip could easily make a chapter in a book, especially the difficulties with the ATVs; crossing swamps, water and windfalls; driving through forests and bush, and, the worst, through tundra over so-called "Negro heads." These are big turf bumps or bulges, up to seventy centimetres in height, one beside the other, which originate due to repeated frost and thawing. The all-terrain vehicle bumped around on the bulges like a balloon, as it was thrown each time to a different angle. The rides gave us the same feeling as a Bronco rider in a rodeo must experience. More than half of our driving was directly around or even through watercourses. Sometimes we crossed the same creek or river more than fifty times a day, so we and our equipment were constantly wet.

It is also hard to provide a short description of the main hunting season. In the middle of August, I got my first guest from New Mexico. We stayed in the valley of Royal Creek and we used the Hondas for transportation. Within ten days, we got a Dall ram and a caribou. Afterwards, Rick moved me by plane about 200 kilometres further to the north by Hart River, where I used a rubber boat, a "Zodiac." My next guest was from Switzerland and I hoped I could communicate with him in German. Unfortunately, he was from the Italian canton, so his main language was Italian, then French, with a little bit of German and English. This was okay, but he was not a good hiker and even worse at shooting. He was very nervous, so I had to finish his two trophy game, a Dall ram and a moose. His friend hunted with me only for one day, when we got a ram The next guest from New Jersey was a slow guy. He moved slowly, he needed time for everything, but he shot fast and inaccurately. He missed a ram five times in one hour. Later he shot several times at a moose, which I had to finish in the middle of a river. I did not have another chance as the moose headed for a large swamp, from which he would be nearly impossible to retrieve. However, the trouble did not finish with my shot. The stream carried the moose along until it finally stopped in shallow water almost exactly opposite our camp. Even so, it was hard to manipulate something as heavy as a seven- to eight-hundred-kilogram moose in water. Initially, I tried to tow the moose with the Zodiac — but in vain. Finally, I had to do all the work in the water. First, I skinned the head, the neck, and the chest. Then I cut the head. All these parts are used for mounting of the trophy. It took me about one hour and I even had to use a chainsaw. Afterwards, the lighter carcass was lifted up by the water and floated about one kilometre with the stream. The next day I finished cutting and dragging the rest of the moose to shore, which took me more than half of a day. A couple of days later we walked near the river and spotted a Dall ram. The guest again missed twice before he finally shot him.

The next guest was from Arizona and he wanted above all to shoot a grizzly. When he finally had a chance, he did not manage it because of his lethargy. It was already the end of September and the weather was miserable. It was very foggy and snow often fell. In this weather we could not hike to look for game, so we loaded the boat and set off with the stream. We floated many kilometres and did not see much game, but we came across a grizzly sow with two cubs, who were swimming in heavy snow across the river. The next day I saw a fine grizzly bear close to a beaver lodge. My guest was muffled up in his clothing and reclined, or even slept, most of the time. When I called his attention to the bear, it took him a long time to wake up, shed his extra clothing and get ready. The bear did not wait and disappeared. Finally, we got a very good moose on the northern boundary of Rick's hunting area. It was about 120 kilometres south of the arctic circle. On the same day, we had prearranged with Rick to pick up the guest for departure. Rick already looked for us, as about ten minutes after the shooting, we heard his plane. The guest departed and I was left with the moose, which was more than a half a kilometre from the river. It was already afternoon and I also had to make camp, so I was not able to finish the moose. I still had enough work for the next day, but there was a heavy frost overnight (–20° Celsius). In the morning, when I tried to find something to warm up from my remaining food, Rick unexpectedly brought another guest. He was an older, retired American, who did not have any urge to go hunting, or even to walk around the camp. He whimpered, could I shoot a moose for him, so he would not fly home empty-handed. I was not enthustiastic as we shot a good older bull, with a 165-inch antler span. So I had to work on two moose, one of them totally frozen. Luckily for me, they were not far apart. It was a very good area for moose and the rut was at its peak. The guest departed the next day and I stayed for two more days. I saw more game, including two other good moose bulls. Big grizzly tracks appeared on my last night, close to camp.

From the Hart River, where I had spent five weeks and travelled about 170 kilometres by water, Rick moved me back to the base camp at Hart Lake. It was already the end of the season, and every day there was snow and frost, so I did not have a chance to have a shower or to do my laundry. I at least changed to cleaner clothes, and I was happy not to be making camp every day or cooking, as Rick's wife, Nancy, did all the cooking in the base camp. However, I got another assignment. We had fourteen horses and we found them five to six kilometres from camp every day, as they had nothing to graze on any closer. Another guide and I each had a guest for a moose hunt near the camp. Every day, we came back wet and half-frozen and started again the next day with fresh hope. The fourth day, the other party got a moose, but my guest and I did not see any. Finally, we met our "lucky" moose and when at last we got a good shot, the plane with the other hunters was overhead, leaving the camp. We missed the plane by a couple of hours. For the next four days there was snow with heavy fog, so we waited in vain to fly out. My guest ran out of cigarettes and shivered at night with cold, but we had no other choice than to wait. Finally, in the middle of October, all the rest of us from the camp managed to get out. I went to Elsa, where I had left my pick-up truck. For the whole summer I had hoped to get to Dawson City, but due to winter weather I had to give up the 200-kilometre detour. I drove directly to Whitehorse, picked up the rest of my stuff from the summer and drove home, through complete winter conditions. I managed the 2,700-kilometre-long drive to Canmore in two days, with only four hours rest.

I left out the details about single hunts, because each one could make a chapter on its own. It is impossible to describe the location of each campsite, whether I stayed a week or just a single night. The whole huge area, where I spent three and a half months; where I slept in a tent and did my bathing and my laundry in lakes, rivers and creeks, is a beautiful country and the real wilderness. There are not huge numbers of game, however I did see about 35 grizzlies, 40 wolves of different colors ranging from white or beige to grey and black, around 250 moose, 200 caribou, 400 Dall sheep and several black bears. I also saw martens, hares, bald and golden eagles, and ptarmigan. The latter probably had a population peak in this year so I saw flocks of about 200 birds by Hart Lake. When their plumage changed to the white color, they looked like white clouds. I found many antlers shed by moose and caribou. Some would be excellent trophies, but due to restricted weight in our plane, I took only one antler home. On Royal Creek, I found ten caribou carcasses with mostly good trophies, probably a result of wolf kills in winter or early spring.

The Yukon is a land with beautiful long and warm days in summer, but also long winters, when the days are very short. As I wrote this account during the winter, I heard that the temperature in Alaska and theYukon fell well below –50° Celsius, some places even to –60 or 70°. The cold spell lasted several weeks, so some hamlets had to be evacuated as the habitants were not able to travel to buy food.

I will never forget the hours spent in small planes, mostly squeezed in, between camping equipment, guns, cans of gas, food boxes, and other necessities, which were always in transit to or from some camp. Many times we landed in the advancing dusk or even in darkness, often in strong wind or in heavy snow. I can still feel the jerking of the plane when it bumps over gravel or over waves on lakes and rivers. Somehow we always managed, and I have to say that Rick was an excellent bush pilot. Once, I saw him take off in late evening, overloaded, as usual, when the wheels had already left a river gravel bar but were still touching water. I also could not forget our wanderings with the Zodiacs on the rivers, which I did not know and how I had to guess from the waves, what was ahead of us. The rubber boats are unsinkable, however, the supplies on the boat get wet easily. It is no pleasure to cook drenched food and even worse to sleep in wet sleeping bags for one who is cold and tired. With one exception, all the hunters were much younger than I, but they mostly complained about the hardships, they slept longer, carried only small packsacks (compared to my own) and did not need to cook. Several times, I was worried that I would not be able to get up the next morning, but it always passed over. We had enough food, especially meat, and though I lost six kilos I felt very well. I could never forget the feeling of being in front of an Alaskan moose. One feels like an ant, especially if the moose is shot and there is only one man to process it. It is hard to forget hours and days spent in the saddle on horses, who know the area. I felt sorry for one experienced horse, who came back to the base camp with a novice a day after the departure of the other horses from Hart Lake camp. We were not able to do anything for them, only to leave them to their fate, alone all winter long. I doubt that they would survive.

It is said that those who spend some time in the north long to come back. I have the same feeling and I hope to come back."

Now, several years later, Petr works regularly as a hunting guide in the Northwest Territories and in northern British Columbia.

20
... and Life Goes On

*"We learned the shocking truth that 'home' isn't necessarily a certain spot on earth. It must be a place where you **feel** at home, which means 'free' to us."* — Marvin A. Trapp

My job was not as exiting as Petr's. In May, I had the successful interview with Banff National Park which gained me a position in the campgrounds. Unfortunately, this was a short-term position, which started late in June and lasted only until September. So I had to work most of time when the children had their holidays and I had to find a way to keep them busy. Kate, herself, took initiative and tried to find a job. She found a position as a kitchen helper in a nearby restaurant. She was proud of her earning ability and the owner and all the restaurant staff were very friendly to her. Anytime that she had to stay late, she got a ride home, even though we did not live far. Tom, encouraged by Kate, also tried to find work. Finally, he found the same position as Kate, but in another restaurant. At first, he liked it very much. The owner allowed employees to have snacks in the restaurant. As Tom had a sweet tooth and preferred desserts, he probably ate more of value than he made in salary. The owner put a stop to snacks after a week, and though Tom was not happy, he stayed. I felt a little sad, when I had to apply for Tom's Social Insurance Number, which allowed him to work at thirteen years. However, it did not hurt him at all, rather it was good for him. Both children gained experience in a different atmosphere and with other people, and they found out for themselves how hard it is to make money.

They had days off in their work that matched with my work schedule, so we were able to spend some time together. The summer was warm and we used our free time for many beautiful trips. Before we went out, we planned everything with maps and tried to fill the gaps in our knowledge ahead of time. We hiked the trails, not only in Banff National Park and Kananaskis Country, but also in Kootenay, Yoho and Jasper National Parks. I bought a membership in the Alpine Club of Canada so we could stay in their huts. Cir always came with us, even if we sometimes had initial troubles with the hut management. But he was quiet and very obedient, so everything was soon solved to the satisfaction of both sides. In the middle of August, the children finished their jobs and went, for a week, to camp with the teepee. This time, we found a place close to the Bow River so they could use a kayak which somebody had given to them. Both Kate and Tom invited a friend to stay for a day with them. Our children loved it, but I am not sure about the other children, who found it hard to make everything for themselves.

For the last week of the summer holiday, I booked Kate and Tom into a horse camp offered through the YMCA. I paid for half and they both paid the other half from their summer earnings, so they would understand why they worked. Campers stayed in teepees, much bigger than our own. Each child got their "own" horse to care for and ride. Besides the daily riding, they had one overnight trip and a "mini rodeo" towards the end of the week. Tom wrote afterwards of his experiences to Petr: "So first we had a short distance ride and I won. Then we had a barrel ride and I was second. Afterwards we had a long distance ride and I again won." He was very proud of his prizes!

For the whole week, I fought the temptation to visit them. When I finally came to pick up them, both Kate and Tom were happy, tanned and they felt only sadness as they had to say good-bye to their new friends and the camp leaders. Unfortunately, they were not able to repeat the camp in the next year, as one-week camps were not offered any more. Instead, there were three-weeks camps, which were too costly, even when we combined our money with the childrens' savings.

My own job did not have many professional requirements. I was glad to make use of my own knowledge about trails and interesting places in Banff National Park whenever visitors needed details. We alternated shifts between working in the information booth, where we sold camping permits, and cleaning the campground. The campground had two sections. The newer section had about 400 sites and the older one, located on a shore of a lake, had only about 80. I liked to work in the old one, where the atmosphere was quiet and I had more time to chat with the visitors.

Some of my co-workers were local people; others were students. I was surprised to find that the shifts with local people were more enjoyable than the ones with students, who tended to view the work as a nuisance. Most of them had worked in the park for several seasons, so they were hired back automatically, in spite of their poor attitude. One of the requirements for the job was self-motivation, but nobody expected to see it. It is, in fact, hard to be motivated in a two- or three-month job. So the students' only motivation was to make money, and that was boring. Working with such people was stressful and I often felt odd about my efforts to feel happy. For myself, I knew that if I would like to feel content with my work, I had to know, at least, that my job was properly done, or to find some small pleasures or details to improve it. The work for Forestry and even Parks was easy for me to enjoy. I was delighted that I had a chance to be outside most of the time and to watch the nature around me. I observed wildflowers, saw elk and deer in the campgrounds and watched the clouds and changes in the landscape depending on the weather. We often laughed with the local people, that tourists pay dearly for such views, so why not enjoy this aspect of our work?

The work in the campground finished in September and, again, I looked for a winter job. Finally, I did the same jobs as last year, working part-time in the hotel and part-time in the school. It was hard to keep my mood positive. Fortunately, the next summer Forestry called me back for another summer job and I worked with them both full- and part-time for the next decade.

Even with our restricted income, we were able to save some money. I wanted to buy a house and move out of the trailer park, as I had never felt truly at home there. We were not accustomed to living on such small lots, squeezed and cramped, where we could easily watch family-life in the other trailers through the windows. At first, living like this was a necessity. However, more and more, I felt discontent, especially in summer when this, the only camping facility in town, was noisy and crowded.

The empty trailers and camping spots filled up quickly in summer. The rows of small trailers, which people parked there year-round and which were mostly empty over winter, were fully occupied. Right by the entrance to the park was a location for group camping. Everywhere, there was noise and the blast of radios. Gangs of children ran through each unfenced lot — and our's was one — without restriction. After all, it was holiday time!

On my walks with our dog, Cir, through different parts of town I would look around at the houses for sale. Especially, the ones with large lots attracted me. I checked the prices but they looked unattainable to me, as I thought about it over and over. House prices went up after the Olympic games, but it did not matter to us. We still did not have enough money to buy a house and Petr did not like the idea of being in debt for years. However, he acknowledged that we needed more room.

In the fall, we abandoned, or rather, postponed, the idea of buying a house. A part of our savings went to pay expenses for our first visitor from Czechoslovakia. Our families, though we continued to write letters, could not decide on such a trip, but Petr invited an old friend, a carver, who had helped Petr to learn this art many years ago to come for a visit. Jura, Petr's friend, was already retired so he was able to easily get a permit for a visit to Canada. He was enthusiastic about Petr's invitation, because it was, for the average Czech citizen, an unusual opportunity. After Petr came back from the Yukon, they travelled together through Alberta and part of British Columbia. They visited some old gold fields and mines to look for semi-precious stones, as this was Jura's hobby. Jura even managed to carve some rifle stocks and cabinets for Petr's friends. Altogether, Jura liked his stay here very much and he often repeated in his letters to us what a wonderful time he had.

In the winter, Petr got a job, which he liked, at the Canmore Nordic Centre in trail maintenance and grooming. Our financial situation improved, so I again started to think about a house. Finally, I persuaded Petr that we would not need to wait for a miracle or anybody's help and that we were able to manage the loan. So towards spring, we started to look for a house. We started at the bottom of the price range and we saw a lot of different houses in Canmore. We checked houses which were falling apart but were located on excellent lots. We looked at cottages and houses where the interior was ruined by transient renters. The good houses which had enough room were usually priced above our budget. Finally, we decided on a modular house, which was located on a spacious corner lot in a quiet area. There were only a few neighbors, and it backed onto the golf course and a recreation area. Across the street was a strip of forest with a pond. The view from the large deck was beautiful and this helped to seal the deal. The yard around the house was not landscaped, but we were able to move in immediately and only minor repairs were needed. We had to change some single-pane windows for double, paint, and change the wallpaper. Again, we were missing a workshop, so Petr built it, his third one in Canada.

Unfortunately, nothing was going easily. We were not able to sell our trailer right away, so we asked friends for a loan for our down-payment. They lent us money without charging any interest or asking for any guarantee, which we deeply appreciated. We rented our trailer to a young couple, who wanted to buy it in a couple of months. To our regret, they just showed us the wrong side of renting. Within three months, they were able to ruin not only my carefully kept garden, but also damaged the inside of the trailer. A year earlier, we had installed a new carpet, which I tried to unsuccessfully to steam clean after the renters left, but the new owners had to change it anyhow. However, after three months, we sold the trailer and repaid the loan to our friends, which left only our mortgage for several years.

Later that year, we had a second visitor from Czechoslovakia. Petr's sister came for two months. She was seriously ill and though she was only just past forty years old, she knew she did not have much time left. Sadly, she lived only another half year after her visit. Afterwards, we appreciated even more that we had a chance to be together and that she enjoyed her stay with us. That summer, Petr and I worked seasonally, but for a longer term. Petr worked at the nordic centre, I had a job with Forestry. Petr had also arranged to work two months as a hunting guide, in the Northwest Territories this time. He left at the end of August, though his sister was still here. I had to carefully plan my days to spend maximum time with her after work. Kate and Tom helped a lot on short trips near Canmore. My sister-in-law, Bozka, was not able to hike, so our trips were tourist-oriented excursions. I rode on the Sulfur Mountain gondola for the first time during her visit and later took several days off to drive with her to Vancouver. Of course, I worried about making such a long trip with her, but the cost of going by plane or train was too great. What she really thought about our accommodation in Vancouver, I did not dare to ask. Searching for an inexpensive hotel, I looked through a travel guide and found one on East Hastings Street. A Vancouver resident would have realized right away what that address meant, but to me, it had no significance. I was a little shocked when I first saw the hotel, but tried not to show my anxiety. I sighed with relief when I saw our room, actually a double one, which was on the sixth floor, well furnished, and very clean. We had a beautiful view of the water and mountains on the north shore. As our floor was quiet, we only needed our courage to go out in the evenings. The painted girls and strange characters on the streets near the hotel gave us a view of life in an environment we had never encountered before. However, we were not bothered as we went out to enjoy our evening walks. When Bozka returned home, most of her memories were pleasant ones, in spite of not always feeling well.

September came, with an early first frost, something almost unknown in Europe. However, the day on which I drove Bozka to the airport was beautiful. The blue Alberta sky seemed like a dome, above the prairie and extending to the mountains. It was close to evening, and the shadows were getting longer as the brown prairie grass took on a pinkish tinge from the sunset. We both were delighted with such a gorgeous day. Bozka, however, was already, in her thoughts, on her homeward trip. Surely, after two months away, she looked forward her return. We talked about it and I started to wonder if I would change places with her. It did not attract me. Quite the opposite, I felt happy that it was not me who had to leave. I was very content to stay and I counted all the blessings which I had here. Surely, this beautiful evening was one of them.

I guess that is the right feeling to have about one's home — to be happy where we live and to desire to stay there.

Epilogue

The same year, 1989, in the early winter, I again volunteered to help with cross-country skiing. Canmore hosted a World Cup and I was chosen as a hostess for the Czechoslovakian team. This time I did not need an interview or any other check, as volunteers did for the Olympics.

Right at the airport, when I welcomed my team, the athletes excitedly asked if I had heard the news from the Eastern Bloc. Of course I had heard that the Berlin Wall was opened in October and presently Czechoslovakia was in the midst of an uprising. Every day, we had listened to the unbelievable news. The communist regime, which looked so hard to break, was suddenly losing its power. The athletes regretted that they would not be present in their country when the communist regime would be overthrown. I still could not believe that could happen, but they were right. In just days, the "Velvet Revolution" prevailed in Czechoslovakia and the old government was defeated. The other socialist countries — Poland, Bulgaria and Romania— also fought for liberation. It did not always go as smoothly as in Czechoslovakia. In Romania, after a difficult fight, the government changed, and the old communist dictator, Caucescu and his wife were executed.

After a couple of weeks, the Czech borders were opened and former escapees were welcome to visit their country of origin. It was something most of us did not even dream of before. Many former Czechoslovak citizens, who presently lived in various countries of the world, went back to visit; some even returned to live there. For me and Petr, it took three more years before we made the trip to visit our families in our old country. It was very pleasant to see familiar places, revisit memories dear to us, and even more enjoyable to meet our families and friends. However, we happily returned to our home, to Canada.

I was even more pleased that our children came to the same kind of feeling on their own. Through the years, they both became more and more involved in sport — Kate in cross-country skiing and Tom in biathlon.

Racing successfully allowed them to travel; first throughout Canada, to places we adults had not yet seen— Nova Scotia, Quebec and even the Northwest Territories. Later, after the "Velvet Revolution," Petr came up with the idea to send Kate and afterwards, Tom, to Czechoslovakia for training in exchange for hosting some Czech athletes here.

So, in the summer of 1990, Kate went to her country of origin to live and train for six weeks with two girls from the junior cross-country ski team. Later, both girls came to Canada. Tom went a year later, also to train, with the Czech Biathlon Team. Of course, the visits were valuable, not just for the training, but also for the chance to experience Czechoslovakia on their own. Both Kate and Tom's spoken Czech language improved significantly. Tom even learned to speak a north Bohemian dialect which we had never used at home. When the World Junior Biathlon Championship was held in Slovakia (a part of Czechoslovakia which peacefully split off in 1992, and which has a language similar enough to Czech to be thought of as a dialect), Tom's language skills were good enough to translate not only for the Canadian team, but also for the Italians, Norwegians, Germans and others intent on making new friends. He was so popular that it was hard to keep up correspondence afterwards with all his new European friends.

A year later, the biathlon coaches persuaded Kate to switch to that sport from cross-country skiing. The junior biathlon team was short of young women and Kate, being a strong skier, would be a good addition to the team. All summer and fall, she trained hard with Petr, who had been volunteering as a biathlon coach for many years, guiding her. Their efforts paid off, as Kate qualified for the World Junior Championship that winter. As Tom also qualified, they travelled together to Rupolding, Germany to race. Of course, Petr and I were proud of them and it was not only us, the Canmore community cherished them and was very supportive.

As for Kate and Tom, they enjoyed their travels but they always returned with the same feeling: they were happy to be back home in Canada!

Eva Zidek was born in Prague, the capital of Czechoslovakia. She studied forestry, a five-year program with the University of Prague. After her schooling, she worked in the field for the Czech Forest Service, as a forest technician and district manager; later as an independent forester for the National Forest Management Institute.

With her work, she moved several times, married, had two children and last lived in Jeseniky, in the north-eastern mountains of Czechoslovakia. Eva worked there in the environmental field, for a Land-Protected Area (similar to a provincial park) as a forester/biologist. There the family came to a fateful decision to flee the country and get to Canada.

In Canada, Eva has worked in various positions, including field work for the Alberta Forest Service. She is presently working for Parks Canada.